Privacy Engineering
Complete Self-Assessment Guide

The guidance in this Self-Assessment is based on Privacy Engineering best practices and standards in business process architecture, design and quality management. The guidance is also based on the professional judgment of the individual collaborators listed in the Acknowledgments.

Notice of rights

Trademarks

Table of Contents

About The Art of Service

The Art of Service, Business Process Architects since 2000, is dedicated to helping stakeholders achieve excellence.

Defining, designing, creating, and implementing a process to solve a stakeholders challenge or meet an objective is the most valuable role… In EVERY group, company, organization and department.

Unless you're talking a one-time, single-use project, there should be a process. Whether that process is managed and implemented by humans, AI, or a combination of the two, it needs to be designed by someone with a complex enough perspective to ask the right questions.

Someone capable of asking the right questions and step back and say, 'What are we really trying to accomplish here? And is there a different way to look at it?'

With The Art of Service's Standard Requirements Self-Assessments, we empower people who can do just that — whether their title is marketer, entrepreneur, manager, salesperson, consultant, Business Process Manager, executive assistant, IT Manager, CIO etc... —they are the people who rule the future. They are people who watch the process as it happens, and ask the right questions to make the process work better.

Contact us when you need any support with this Self-Assessment and any help with templates, blue-prints and examples of standard documents you might need:

http://theartofservice.com
service@theartofservice.com

Included Resources - how to access

Included with your purchase of the book is the Privacy

Engineering Self-Assessment Spreadsheet Dashboard which contains all questions and Self-Assessment areas and auto-generates insights, graphs, and project RACI planning - all with examples to get you started right away.

How? Simply send an email to
access@theartofservice.com
with this books' title in the subject to get the Privacy Engineering Self Assessment Tool right away.

You will receive the following contents with New and Updated specific criteria:

- The latest quick edition of the book in PDF

- The latest complete edition of the book in PDF, which criteria correspond to the criteria in...

- The Self-Assessment Excel Dashboard, and...

- Example pre-filled Self-Assessment Excel Dashboard to get familiar with results generation

- In-depth specific Checklists covering the topic

- Project management checklists and templates to assist with implementation

Purpose of this Self-Assessment

This Self-Assessment has been developed to improve understanding of the requirements and elements of Privacy Engineering, based on best practices and standards in business process architecture, design and quality management.

It is designed to allow for a rapid Self-Assessment to determine how closely existing management practices and procedures correspond to the elements of the Self-Assessment.

The criteria of requirements and elements of Privacy Engineering have been rephrased in the format of a Self-Assessment questionnaire, with a seven-criterion scoring system, as explained in this document.

In this format, even with limited background knowledge of Privacy Engineering, a manager can quickly review existing operations to determine how they measure up to the standards. This in turn can serve as the starting point of a 'gap analysis' to identify management tools or system elements that might usefully be implemented in the organization to help improve overall performance.

How to use the Self-Assessment

On the following pages are a series of questions to identify to what extent your Privacy Engineering initiative is complete in comparison to the requirements set in standards.

To facilitate answering the questions, there is a space in front of each question to enter a score on a scale of '1' to '5'.

1 Strongly Disagree

2 Disagree

3 Neutral

4 Agree

5 Strongly Agree

Read the question and rate it with the following in front of mind:

'In my belief,
the answer to this question is clearly defined'.

There are two ways in which you can choose to interpret this statement;
1. how aware are you that the answer to the question is clearly defined
2. for more in-depth analysis you can choose to gather evidence and confirm the answer to the question. This obviously will take more time, most Self-Assessment users opt for the first way to interpret the question and dig deeper later on based on the outcome of the overall Self-Assessment.

A score of '1' would mean that the answer is not clear at all, where a '5' would mean the answer is crystal clear and defined. Leave emtpy when the question is not applicable or you don't want to answer it, you can skip it without affecting your score. Write your score in the space provided.

After you have responded to all the appropriate statements in each section, compute your average score for that section, using the formula provided, and round to the nearest tenth. Then transfer to the corresponding spoke in the Privacy Engineering Scorecard on the second next page of the Self-Assessment.

Your completed Privacy Engineering Scorecard will give you a clear presentation of which Privacy Engineering areas need attention.

Privacy Engineering
Scorecard Example

Example of how the finalized Scorecard can look like:

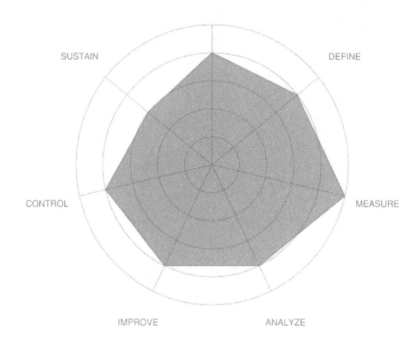

Privacy Engineering Scorecard

Your Scores:

BEGINNING OF THE
SELF-ASSESSMENT:

CRITERION #1: RECOGNIZE

INTENT: Be aware of the need for change. Recognize that there is an unfavorable variation, problem or symptom.

In my belief, the answer to this question is clearly defined:

5 Strongly Agree

4 Agree

3 Neutral

2 Disagree

1 Strongly Disagree

1. How are training requirements identified?
<--- Score

2. What creative shifts do you need to take?
<--- Score

3. How are the privacy engineering's objectives aligned to the group's overall stakeholder strategy?
<--- Score

4. Who else hopes to benefit from it?
<--- Score

5. What is the smallest subset of the problem you can usefully solve?
<--- Score

6. What is the privacy engineering problem definition? What do you need to resolve?
<--- Score

7. What information do users need?
<--- Score

8. What else needs to be measured?
<--- Score

9. Are losses recognized in a timely manner?
<--- Score

10. How can auditing be a preventative security measure?
<--- Score

11. Did you miss any major privacy engineering issues?
<--- Score

12. How do you recognize an privacy engineering objection?
<--- Score

13. What privacy engineering events should you attend?
<--- Score

14. Are your goals realistic? Do you need to redefine your problem? Perhaps the problem has changed or maybe you have reached your goal and need to set a new one?
<--- Score

15. Will a response program recognize when a crisis occurs and provide some level of response?
<--- Score

16. Who needs what information?
<--- Score

17. What resources or support might you need?
<--- Score

18. What do you need to start doing?
<--- Score

19. What are your needs in relation to privacy engineering skills, labor, equipment, and markets?
<--- Score

20. Are employees recognized for desired behaviors?
<--- Score

21. Looking at each person individually – does every one have the qualities which are needed to work in this group?
<--- Score

22. To what extent does each concerned units management team recognize privacy engineering as an effective investment?
<--- Score

23. What are the expected benefits of privacy engineering to the stakeholder?
<--- Score

24. Who should resolve the privacy engineering issues?
<--- Score

25. As a sponsor, customer or management, how important is it to meet goals, objectives?
<--- Score

26. What would happen if privacy engineering weren't done?
<--- Score

27. How do you identify the kinds of information that you will need?
<--- Score

28. Do you know what you need to know about privacy engineering?
<--- Score

29. Consider your own privacy engineering project, what types of organizational problems do you think might be causing or affecting your problem, based on the work done so far?
<--- Score

30. How do you take a forward-looking perspective in identifying privacy engineering research related to market response and models?
<--- Score

31. What situation(s) led to this privacy engineering Self Assessment?
<--- Score

32. Where is training needed?
<--- Score

33. Are controls defined to recognize and contain problems?
<--- Score

34. Can management personnel recognize the monetary benefit of privacy engineering?
<--- Score

35. Why is this needed?
<--- Score

36. Are there regulatory / compliance issues?
<--- Score

37. How are you going to measure success?
<--- Score

38. Why the need?
<--- Score

39. Think about the people you identified for your privacy engineering project and the project responsibilities you would assign to them, what kind of training do you think they would need to perform these responsibilities effectively?
<--- Score

40. What training and capacity building actions are needed to implement proposed reforms?

<--- Score

41. What privacy engineering problem should be solved?
<--- Score

42. Have you identified your privacy engineering key performance indicators?
<--- Score

43. How do you identify subcontractor relationships?
<--- Score

44. Are there any specific expectations or concerns about the privacy engineering team, privacy engineering itself?
<--- Score

45. Are there privacy engineering problems defined?
<--- Score

46. Does your organization need more privacy engineering education?
<--- Score

47. How do you assess your privacy engineering workforce capability and capacity needs, including skills, competencies, and staffing levels?
<--- Score

48. What needs to stay?
<--- Score

49. Whom do you really need or want to serve?
<--- Score

50. Is the quality assurance team identified?
<--- Score

51. Will privacy engineering deliverables need to be tested and, if so, by whom?
<--- Score

52. Are employees recognized or rewarded for performance that demonstrates the highest levels of integrity?
<--- Score

53. Who defines the rules in relation to any given issue?
<--- Score

54. What activities does the governance board need to consider?
<--- Score

55. What is the problem and/or vulnerability?
<--- Score

56. Where do you need to exercise leadership?
<--- Score

57. When a privacy engineering manager recognizes a problem, what options are available?
<--- Score

58. Which needs are not included or involved?
<--- Score

59. What problems are you facing and how do you consider privacy engineering will circumvent those obstacles?

<--- Score

60. Are you dealing with any of the same issues today as yesterday? What can you do about this?
<--- Score

61. What tools and technologies are needed for a custom privacy engineering project?
<--- Score

62. Would you recognize a threat from the inside?
<--- Score

63. Are there any revenue recognition issues?
<--- Score

64. Is the need for organizational change recognized?
<--- Score

65. Do you have/need 24-hour access to key personnel?
<--- Score

66. Who needs to know about privacy engineering?
<--- Score

67. For your privacy engineering project, identify and describe the business environment, is there more than one layer to the business environment?
<--- Score

68. What are the clients issues and concerns?
<--- Score

69. Do you need to avoid or amend any privacy engineering activities?

<--- Score

70. What are the stakeholder objectives to be achieved with privacy engineering?
<--- Score

71. How does it fit into your organizational needs and tasks?
<--- Score

72. What is the recognized need?
<--- Score

73. Which information does the privacy engineering business case need to include?
<--- Score

74. Are there recognized privacy engineering problems?
<--- Score

75. Will it solve real problems?
<--- Score

76. How do you recognize an objection?
<--- Score

77. What privacy engineering capabilities do you need?
<--- Score

78. What should be considered when identifying available resources, constraints, and deadlines?
<--- Score

79. What extra resources will you need?

<--- Score

80. What privacy engineering coordination do you need?
<--- Score

81. Will new equipment/products be required to facilitate privacy engineering delivery, for example is new software needed?
<--- Score

82. What is the extent or complexity of the privacy engineering problem?
<--- Score

83. How much are sponsors, customers, partners, stakeholders involved in privacy engineering? In other words, what are the risks, if privacy engineering does not deliver successfully?
<--- Score

84. What is the problem or issue?
<--- Score

85. How many trainings, in total, are needed?
<--- Score

86. What does privacy engineering success mean to the stakeholders?
<--- Score

87. Do you recognize privacy engineering achievements?
<--- Score

88. What are the privacy engineering resources

needed?
<--- Score

89. What prevents you from making the changes
you know will make you a more effective privacy
engineering leader?
<--- Score

90. Who needs budgets?
<--- Score

91. Who needs to know?
<--- Score

92. What needs to be done?
<--- Score

93. Which issues are too important to ignore?
<--- Score

94. Do you need different information or graphics?
<--- Score

95. Is it needed?
<--- Score

Add up total points for this section:
_ _ _ _ _ = Total points for this section

Divided by: _ _ _ _ _ _ (number of
statements answered) = _ _ _ _ _ _
Average score for this section

Transfer your score to the privacy
engineering Index at the beginning of
the Self-Assessment.

CRITERION #2: DEFINE:

INTENT: Formulate the stakeholder problem. Define the problem, needs and objectives.

In my belief, the answer to this question is clearly defined:

5 Strongly Agree

4 Agree

3 Neutral

2 Disagree

1 Strongly Disagree

1. What is the definition of success?
<--- Score

2. Is the privacy engineering scope manageable?
<--- Score

3. Scope of sensitive information?
<--- Score

4. Who is gathering information?
<--- Score

5. Is scope creep really all bad news?
<--- Score

6. What are the requirements for audit information?
<--- Score

7. How do you keep key subject matter experts in the loop?
<--- Score

8. What scope to assess?
<--- Score

9. What are the privacy engineering tasks and definitions?
<--- Score

10. When are meeting minutes sent out? Who is on the distribution list?
<--- Score

11. Is the current 'as is' process being followed? If not, what are the discrepancies?
<--- Score

12. Will team members perform privacy engineering work when assigned and in a timely fashion?
<--- Score

13. What gets examined?
<--- Score

14. Has anyone else (internal or external to the group)

attempted to solve this problem or a similar one before? If so, what knowledge can be leveraged from these previous efforts?

<--- Score

15. Is there a completed, verified, and validated high-level 'as is' (not 'should be' or 'could be') stakeholder process map?

<--- Score

16. What are the record-keeping requirements of privacy engineering activities?

<--- Score

17. Has the privacy engineering work been fairly and/or equitably divided and delegated among team members who are qualified and capable to perform the work? Has everyone contributed?

<--- Score

18. What defines best in class?

<--- Score

19. Are customer(s) identified and segmented according to their different needs and requirements?

<--- Score

20. Has the improvement team collected the 'voice of the customer' (obtained feedback – qualitative and quantitative)?

<--- Score

21. Are all requirements met?

<--- Score

22. Is there a completed SIPOC representation,

describing the Suppliers, Inputs, Process, Outputs, and Customers?
<--- Score

23. The political context: who holds power?
<--- Score

24. Is the scope of privacy engineering defined?
<--- Score

25. Is the team equipped with available and reliable resources?
<--- Score

26. How do you manage changes in privacy engineering requirements?
<--- Score

27. How and when will the baselines be defined?
<--- Score

28. Is privacy engineering required?
<--- Score

29. Has a privacy engineering requirement not been met?
<--- Score

30. How can the value of privacy engineering be defined?
<--- Score

31. Who is gathering privacy engineering information?
<--- Score

32. What is the scope of the privacy engineering effort?
<--- Score

33. Are there different segments of customers?
<--- Score

34. What knowledge or experience is required?
<--- Score

35. What key stakeholder process output measure(s) does privacy engineering leverage and how?
<--- Score

36. Have all basic functions of privacy engineering been defined?
<--- Score

37. Are audit criteria, scope, frequency and methods defined?
<--- Score

38. What sources do you use to gather information for a privacy engineering study?
<--- Score

39. Do the problem and goal statements meet the SMART criteria (specific, measurable, attainable, relevant, and time-bound)?
<--- Score

40. What is the scope of privacy engineering?
<--- Score

41. Do you have organizational privacy requirements?
<--- Score

42. How do you gather requirements?
<--- Score

43. Who are the privacy engineering improvement team members, including Management Leads and Coaches?
<--- Score

44. What are the core elements of the privacy engineering business case?
<--- Score

45. What was the context?
<--- Score

46. In what way can you redefine the criteria of choice clients have in your category in your favor?
<--- Score

47. Why are you doing privacy engineering and what is the scope?
<--- Score

48. How often are the team meetings?
<--- Score

49. Are roles and responsibilities formally defined?
<--- Score

50. Does the scope remain the same?
<--- Score

51. Has your scope been defined?
<--- Score

52. Will team members regularly document their privacy engineering work?
<--- Score

53. What information do you gather?
<--- Score

54. Is the privacy engineering scope complete and appropriately sized?
<--- Score

55. Is data collected and displayed to better understand customer(s) critical needs and requirements.
<--- Score

56. How do you gather the stories?
<--- Score

57. How do you hand over privacy engineering context?
<--- Score

58. Are the privacy engineering requirements testable?
<--- Score

59. What system do you use for gathering privacy engineering information?
<--- Score

60. How do you build the right business case?
<--- Score

61. What baselines are required to be defined and managed?

<--- Score

62. Are different versions of process maps needed to account for the different types of inputs?
<--- Score

63. What information should you gather?
<--- Score

64. Are required metrics defined, what are they?
<--- Score

65. Are improvement team members fully trained on privacy engineering?
<--- Score

66. What customer feedback methods were used to solicit their input?
<--- Score

67. Is the improvement team aware of the different versions of a process: what they think it is vs. what it actually is vs. what it should be vs. what it could be?
<--- Score

68. Are accountability and ownership for privacy engineering clearly defined?
<--- Score

69. What is in the scope and what is not in scope?
<--- Score

70. What are the privacy engineering use cases?
<--- Score

71. How would you define the culture at your

organization, how susceptible is it to privacy engineering changes?
<--- Score

72. Has a project plan, Gantt chart, or similar been developed/completed?
<--- Score

73. What would be the goal or target for a privacy engineering's improvement team?
<--- Score

74. Is there a critical path to deliver privacy engineering results?
<--- Score

75. Are task requirements clearly defined?
<--- Score

76. What privacy engineering requirements should be gathered?
<--- Score

77. Have specific policy objectives been defined?
<--- Score

78. Are stakeholder processes mapped?
<--- Score

79. Have all of the relationships been defined properly?
<--- Score

80. What scope do you want your strategy to cover?
<--- Score

81. What are the compelling stakeholder reasons for embarking on privacy engineering?
<--- Score

82. What is the context?
<--- Score

83. Do you all define privacy engineering in the same way?
<--- Score

84. Is the work to date meeting requirements?
<--- Score

85. What happens if privacy engineering's scope changes?
<--- Score

86. Is there a clear privacy engineering case definition?
<--- Score

87. Has/have the customer(s) been identified?
<--- Score

88. How will variation in the actual durations of each activity be dealt with to ensure that the expected privacy engineering results are met?
<--- Score

89. If substitutes have been appointed, have they been briefed on the privacy engineering goals and received regular communications as to the progress to date?
<--- Score

90. Are approval levels defined for contracts and supplements to contracts?
<--- Score

91. What are the rough order estimates on cost savings/opportunities that privacy engineering brings?
<--- Score

92. What constraints exist that might impact the team?
<--- Score

93. What is the scope of the privacy engineering work?
<--- Score

94. What is the definition of privacy engineering excellence?
<--- Score

95. Are resources adequate for the scope?
<--- Score

96. What privacy engineering services do you require?
<--- Score

97. How is the team tracking and documenting its work?
<--- Score

98. Who defines (or who defined) the rules and roles?
<--- Score

99. What sort of initial information to gather?
<--- Score

100. Is there regularly 100% attendance at the team meetings? If not, have appointed substitutes attended to preserve cross-functionality and full representation?
<--- Score

101. What specifically is the problem? Where does it occur? When does it occur? What is its extent?
<--- Score

102. How have you defined all privacy engineering requirements first?
<--- Score

103. Is privacy engineering linked to key stakeholder goals and objectives?
<--- Score

104. Does the team have regular meetings?
<--- Score

105. What are the dynamics of the communication plan?
<--- Score

106. How will the privacy engineering team and the group measure complete success of privacy engineering?
<--- Score

107. Where can you gather more information?
<--- Score

108. Is the team sponsored by a champion or stakeholder leader?

<--- Score

109. What are the boundaries of the scope? What is in bounds and what is not? What is the start point? What is the stop point?
<--- Score

110. What is out-of-scope initially?
<--- Score

111. How does the privacy engineering manager ensure against scope creep?
<--- Score

112. How are consistent privacy engineering definitions important?
<--- Score

113. Will a privacy engineering production readiness review be required?
<--- Score

114. How was the 'as is' process map developed, reviewed, verified and validated?
<--- Score

115. Is the team formed and are team leaders (Coaches and Management Leads) assigned?
<--- Score

116. What critical content must be communicated – who, what, when, where, and how?
<--- Score

117. When is the estimated completion date?
<--- Score

118. Is full participation by members in regularly held team meetings guaranteed?
<--- Score

119. Has a team charter been developed and communicated?
<--- Score

120. When is/was the privacy engineering start date?
<--- Score

121. Have the customer needs been translated into specific, measurable requirements? How?
<--- Score

122. Has a high-level 'as is' process map been completed, verified and validated?
<--- Score

123. How do you manage unclear privacy engineering requirements?
<--- Score

124. Is there a privacy engineering management charter, including stakeholder case, problem and goal statements, scope, milestones, roles and responsibilities, communication plan?
<--- Score

125. Do you have a privacy engineering success story or case study ready to tell and share?
<--- Score

126. Has everyone on the team, including the team leaders, been properly trained?

<--- Score

127. Is the team adequately staffed with the desired cross-functionality? If not, what additional resources are available to the team?
<--- Score

128. What are (control) requirements for privacy engineering Information?
<--- Score

129. Who approved the privacy engineering scope?
<--- Score

130. What is in scope?
<--- Score

131. How did the privacy engineering manager receive input to the development of a privacy engineering improvement plan and the estimated completion dates/times of each activity?
<--- Score

132. How do you catch privacy engineering definition inconsistencies?
<--- Score

133. What are the Roles and Responsibilities for each team member and its leadership? Where is this documented?
<--- Score

134. Are there any constraints known that bear on the ability to perform privacy engineering work? How is the team addressing them?
<--- Score

135. How do you gather privacy engineering requirements?
<--- Score

136. How do you manage scope?
<--- Score

137. Is there any additional privacy engineering definition of success?
<--- Score

138. Has the direction changed at all during the course of privacy engineering? If so, when did it change and why?
<--- Score

139. How would you define privacy engineering leadership?
<--- Score

140. What are the tasks and definitions?
<--- Score

141. Is privacy engineering currently on schedule according to the plan?
<--- Score

Add up total points for this section:
_ _ _ _ _ = Total points for this section

Divided by: _ _ _ _ _ _ (number of statements answered) = _ _ _ _ _ _
Average score for this section

Transfer your score to the privacy

engineering Index at the beginning of
the Self-Assessment.

CRITERION #3: MEASURE:

INTENT: Gather the correct data.
Measure the current performance and
evolution of the situation.

In my belief, the answer to this
question is clearly defined:

5 Strongly Agree

4 Agree

3 Neutral

2 Disagree

1 Strongly Disagree

1. Are actual costs in line with budgeted costs?
<--- Score

2. Are missed privacy engineering opportunities
costing your organization money?
<--- Score

3. Have you included everything in your privacy
engineering cost models?

<--- Score

4. Which measures and indicators matter?
<--- Score

5. How will measures be used to manage and adapt?
<--- Score

6. Where can you go to verify the info?
<--- Score

7. What measurements are being captured?
<--- Score

8. How to cause the change?
<--- Score

9. What details are required of the privacy engineering cost structure?
<--- Score

10. What disadvantage does this cause for the user?
<--- Score

11. How will you measure success?
<--- Score

12. What are hidden privacy engineering quality costs?
<--- Score

13. How do you stay flexible and focused to recognize larger privacy engineering results?
<--- Score

14. What are the operational costs after privacy

engineering deployment?
<--- Score

15. How can you reduce costs?
<--- Score

16. What would be a real cause for concern?
<--- Score

17. What are the privacy engineering investment costs?
<--- Score

18. What are your customers expectations and measures?
<--- Score

19. How will your organization measure success?
<--- Score

20. What is measured? Why?
<--- Score

21. What is the cause of any privacy engineering gaps?
<--- Score

22. How do you prevent mis-estimating cost?
<--- Score

23. How can you manage cost down?
<--- Score

24. What are your primary costs, revenues, assets?
<--- Score

25. What is the total fixed cost?
<--- Score

26. When are costs are incurred?
<--- Score

27. How do you measure success?
<--- Score

28. How do you verify the authenticity of the data and information used?
<--- Score

29. What methods are feasible and acceptable to estimate the impact of reforms?
<--- Score

30. How is performance measured?
<--- Score

31. Will privacy engineering have an impact on current business continuity, disaster recovery processes and/or infrastructure?
<--- Score

32. At what cost?
<--- Score

33. Where is the cost?
<--- Score

34. Have you made assumptions about the shape of the future, particularly its impact on your customers and competitors?
<--- Score

35. What measurements are possible, practicable and meaningful?
<--- Score

36. What can be used to verify compliance?
<--- Score

37. Do you have a flow diagram of what happens?
<--- Score

38. What are the uncertainties surrounding estimates of impact?
<--- Score

39. What does your operating model cost?
<--- Score

40. How do you measure lifecycle phases?
<--- Score

41. How do you verify the privacy engineering requirements quality?
<--- Score

42. Are the privacy engineering benefits worth its costs?
<--- Score

43. What could cause you to change course?
<--- Score

44. What is the privacy engineering business impact?
<--- Score

45. What happens if cost savings do not materialize?
<--- Score

46. How do you verify and develop ideas and innovations?
<--- Score

47. What does a Test Case verify?
<--- Score

48. How are you verifying it?
<--- Score

49. Who is involved in verifying compliance?
<--- Score

50. Does the privacy engineering task fit the client's priorities?
<--- Score

51. Is there an opportunity to verify requirements?
<--- Score

52. Are there measurements based on task performance?
<--- Score

53. Have design-to-cost goals been established?
<--- Score

54. What is an unallowable cost?
<--- Score

55. How do you focus on what is right -not who is right?
<--- Score

56. How frequently do you track privacy engineering

measures?
<--- Score

57. Do the benefits outweigh the costs?
<--- Score

58. How can you measure privacy engineering in a systematic way?
<--- Score

59. Is the cost worth the privacy engineering effort ?
<--- Score

60. What are the estimated costs of proposed changes?
<--- Score

61. Are the units of measure consistent?
<--- Score

62. Was a business case (cost/benefit) developed?
<--- Score

63. How is progress measured?
<--- Score

64. What is the total cost related to deploying privacy engineering, including any consulting or professional services?
<--- Score

65. How can you measure the performance?
<--- Score

66. What do you measure and why?
<--- Score

67. What would it cost to replace your technology?
<--- Score

68. What could cause delays in the schedule?
<--- Score

69. How will effects be measured?
<--- Score

70. What is your privacy engineering quality cost segregation study?
<--- Score

71. What causes investor action?
<--- Score

72. How will costs be allocated?
<--- Score

73. What are the types and number of measures to use?
<--- Score

74. What are your operating costs?
<--- Score

75. How long to keep data and how to manage retention costs?
<--- Score

76. How sensitive must the privacy engineering strategy be to cost?
<--- Score

77. How do you verify privacy engineering

completeness and accuracy?
<--- Score

78. What are the strategic priorities for this year?
<--- Score

79. How do you verify your resources?
<--- Score

80. What are you verifying?
<--- Score

81. Are privacy engineering vulnerabilities categorized and prioritized?
<--- Score

82. What are the costs and benefits?
<--- Score

83. Is the solution cost-effective?
<--- Score

84. How do you measure variability?
<--- Score

85. What does verifying compliance entail?
<--- Score

86. What are allowable costs?
<--- Score

87. Are the measurements objective?
<--- Score

88. What are the costs of delaying privacy engineering action?

<--- Score

89. When a disaster occurs, who gets priority?
<--- Score

90. Who should receive measurement reports?
<--- Score

91. How will you measure your privacy engineering effectiveness?
<--- Score

92. What does losing customers cost your organization?
<--- Score

93. Where is it measured?
<--- Score

94. How are measurements made?
<--- Score

95. Is it possible to estimate the impact of unanticipated complexity such as wrong or failed assumptions, feedback, etcetera on proposed reforms?
<--- Score

96. Why do the measurements/indicators matter?
<--- Score

97. Why a privacy engineering focus?
<--- Score

98. What evidence is there and what is measured?
<--- Score

99. Are indirect costs charged to the privacy engineering program?
<--- Score

100. What causes innovation to fail or succeed in your organization?
<--- Score

101. What harm might be caused?
<--- Score

102. How is the value delivered by privacy engineering being measured?
<--- Score

103. Among the privacy engineering product and service cost to be estimated, which is considered hardest to estimate?
<--- Score

104. What is your decision requirements diagram?
<--- Score

105. What are the current costs of the privacy engineering process?
<--- Score

106. Did you tackle the cause or the symptom?
<--- Score

107. What causes mismanagement?
<--- Score

108. How will success or failure be measured?
<--- Score

109. What is the root cause(s) of the problem?
<--- Score

110. What do people want to verify?
<--- Score

111. What causes extra work or rework?
<--- Score

112. How do you aggregate measures across priorities?
<--- Score

113. What are the privacy engineering key cost drivers?
<--- Score

114. Do you effectively measure and reward individual and team performance?
<--- Score

115. Are supply costs steady or fluctuating?
<--- Score

116. What tests verify requirements?
<--- Score

117. What are your key privacy engineering organizational performance measures, including key short and longer-term financial measures?
<--- Score

118. What relevant entities could be measured?
<--- Score

119. Which costs should be taken into account?
<--- Score

120. Are there any easy-to-implement alternatives to privacy engineering? Sometimes other solutions are available that do not require the cost implications of a full-blown project?
<--- Score

121. Do you have an issue in getting priority?
<--- Score

122. Are you aware of what could cause a problem?
<--- Score

123. How do you verify performance?
<--- Score

124. What are the costs?
<--- Score

125. Who pays the cost?
<--- Score

126. How do you verify if privacy engineering is built right?
<--- Score

127. What drives O&M cost?
<--- Score

128. How do you quantify and qualify impacts?
<--- Score

129. Is a follow-up focused external privacy engineering review required?

<--- Score

130. Does a privacy engineering quantification method exist?
<--- Score

131. Are you able to realize any cost savings?
<--- Score

132. Do you verify that corrective actions were taken?
<--- Score

133. Do you have any cost privacy engineering limitation requirements?
<--- Score

134. What users will be impacted?
<--- Score

135. What are the costs of reform?
<--- Score

136. How do you control the overall costs of your work processes?
<--- Score

137. Why do you expend time and effort to implement measurement, for whom?
<--- Score

138. Do you aggressively reward and promote the people who have the biggest impact on creating excellent privacy engineering services/products?
<--- Score

139. How do you measure efficient delivery of privacy

engineering services?

<--- Score

140. How do your measurements capture actionable privacy engineering information for use in exceeding your customers expectations and securing your customers engagement?

<--- Score

141. Does management have the right priorities among projects?

<--- Score

Add up total points for this section:
_____ = Total points for this section

Divided by: _____ (number of
statements answered) = _____
Average score for this section

Transfer your score to the privacy
engineering Index at the beginning of
the Self-Assessment.

CRITERION #4: ANALYZE:

INTENT: Analyze causes, assumptions and hypotheses.

In my belief, the answer to this question is clearly defined:

5 Strongly Agree

4 Agree

3 Neutral

2 Disagree

1 Strongly Disagree

1. How is the privacy engineering Value Stream Mapping managed?
<--- Score

2. Is the final output clearly identified?
<--- Score

3. How do you promote understanding that opportunity for improvement is not criticism of the status quo, or the people who created the status quo?

<--- Score

4. Do your contracts/agreements contain data security obligations?
<--- Score

5. Who has access to your data?
<--- Score

6. How do you ensure that the privacy engineering opportunity is realistic?
<--- Score

7. Were Pareto charts (or similar) used to portray the 'heavy hitters' (or key sources of variation)?
<--- Score

8. What tools were used to generate the list of possible causes?
<--- Score

9. What is the output?
<--- Score

10. Do staff qualifications match your project?
<--- Score

11. Was a detailed process map created to amplify critical steps of the 'as is' stakeholder process?
<--- Score

12. Are all staff in core privacy engineering subjects Highly Qualified?
<--- Score

13. How does the organization define, manage, and

improve its privacy engineering processes?
<--- Score

14. How can risk management be tied procedurally to process elements?
<--- Score

15. Is the performance gap determined?
<--- Score

16. What, related to, privacy engineering processes does your organization outsource?
<--- Score

17. What are evaluation criteria for the output?
<--- Score

18. Have you defined which data is gathered how?
<--- Score

19. Where is the data?
<--- Score

20. Can you add value to the current privacy engineering decision-making process (largely qualitative) by incorporating uncertainty modeling (more quantitative)?
<--- Score

21. Identify an operational issue in your organization, for example, could a particular task be done more quickly or more efficiently by privacy engineering?
<--- Score

22. What internal processes need improvement?
<--- Score

23. How will the data be checked for quality?
<--- Score

24. What data do you need to collect?
<--- Score

25. Is pre-qualification of suppliers carried out?
<--- Score

26. Is there a strict change management process?
<--- Score

27. How has the privacy engineering data been gathered?
<--- Score

28. How will corresponding data be collected?
<--- Score

29. What are your best practices for minimizing privacy engineering project risk, while demonstrating incremental value and quick wins throughout the privacy engineering project lifecycle?
<--- Score

30. What are the revised rough estimates of the financial savings/opportunity for privacy engineering improvements?
<--- Score

31. Are privacy engineering changes recognized early enough to be approved through the regular process?
<--- Score

32. What is the complexity of the output produced?

<--- Score

33. Has an output goal been set?
<--- Score

34. Where is the data coming from to measure compliance?
<--- Score

35. What conclusions were drawn from the team's data collection and analysis? How did the team reach these conclusions?
<--- Score

36. What privacy engineering data should be managed?
<--- Score

37. Record-keeping requirements flow from the records needed as inputs, outputs, controls and for transformation of a privacy engineering process, are the records needed as inputs to the privacy engineering process available?
<--- Score

38. What privacy engineering data do you gather or use now?
<--- Score

39. How many input/output points does it require?
<--- Score

40. Is the required privacy engineering data gathered?
<--- Score

41. Do quality systems drive continuous

improvement?
<--- Score

42. What training and qualifications will you need?
<--- Score

43. Which privacy engineering data should be retained?
<--- Score

44. Who is involved in the management review process?
<--- Score

45. How are outputs preserved and protected?
<--- Score

46. What privacy engineering data will be collected?
<--- Score

47. What is the oversight process?
<--- Score

48. How is privacy engineering data gathered?
<--- Score

49. Were there any improvement opportunities identified from the process analysis?
<--- Score

50. How much data can be collected in the given timeframe?
<--- Score

51. What successful thing are you doing today that may be blinding you to new growth opportunities?

<--- Score

52. What types of data do your privacy engineering indicators require?
<--- Score

53. Think about some of the processes you undertake within your organization, which do you own?
<--- Score

54. How do you measure the operational performance of your key work systems and processes, including productivity, cycle time, and other appropriate measures of process effectiveness, efficiency, and innovation?
<--- Score

55. What is the Value Stream Mapping?
<--- Score

56. Is the suppliers process defined and controlled?
<--- Score

57. What are the privacy engineering business drivers?
<--- Score

58. How do mission and objectives affect the privacy engineering processes of your organization?
<--- Score

59. What are your key performance measures or indicators and in-process measures for the control and improvement of your privacy engineering processes?
<--- Score

60. Has data output been validated?
<--- Score

61. What tools were used to narrow the list of possible causes?
<--- Score

62. How do you identify specific privacy engineering investment opportunities and emerging trends?
<--- Score

63. Where is privacy engineering data gathered?
<--- Score

64. How is the data gathered?
<--- Score

65. What privacy engineering data should be collected?
<--- Score

66. What are the best opportunities for value improvement?
<--- Score

67. When should a process be art not science?
<--- Score

68. How is the way you as the leader think and process information affecting your organizational culture?
<--- Score

69. What other jobs or tasks affect the performance of the steps in the privacy engineering process?
<--- Score

70. What were the crucial 'moments of truth' on the process map?
<--- Score

71. What process should you select for improvement?
<--- Score

72. Is the requester the data subject?
<--- Score

73. Do several people in different organizational units assist with the privacy engineering process?
<--- Score

74. Was a cause-and-effect diagram used to explore the different types of causes (or sources of variation)?
<--- Score

75. Is the privacy engineering process severely broken such that a re-design is necessary?
<--- Score

76. What output to create?
<--- Score

77. What is the privacy engineering Driver?
<--- Score

78. Do you, as a leader, bounce back quickly from setbacks?
<--- Score

79. How do you implement and manage your work processes to ensure that they meet design requirements?
<--- Score

80. What data is gathered?
<--- Score

81. What are your privacy engineering processes?
<--- Score

82. Where can you get qualified talent today?
<--- Score

83. Who will gather what data?
<--- Score

84. Are all team members qualified for all tasks?
<--- Score

85. What did the team gain from developing a sub-process map?
<--- Score

86. What are your current levels and trends in key privacy engineering measures or indicators of product and process performance that are important to and directly serve your customers?
<--- Score

87. What does the data say about the performance of the stakeholder process?
<--- Score

88. What information qualified as important?
<--- Score

89. Who will facilitate the team and process?
<--- Score

90. How do your work systems and key work processes relate to and capitalize on your core competencies?
<--- Score

91. What other organizational variables, such as reward systems or communication systems, affect the performance of this privacy engineering process?
<--- Score

92. Are your outputs consistent?
<--- Score

93. Do you have the authority to produce the output?
<--- Score

94. What quality tools were used to get through the analyze phase?
<--- Score

95. Who qualifies to gain access to data?
<--- Score

96. Who gets your output?
<--- Score

97. Think about the functions involved in your privacy engineering project, what processes flow from these functions?
<--- Score

98. What resources go in to get the desired output?
<--- Score

99. Is data and process analysis, root cause analysis and quantifying the gap/opportunity in place?

<--- Score

100. How difficult is it to qualify what privacy engineering ROI is?
<--- Score

101. What will drive privacy engineering change?
<--- Score

102. What qualifications and skills do you need?
<--- Score

103. What kind of crime could a potential new hire have committed that would not only not disqualify him/her from being hired by your organization, but would actually indicate that he/she might be a particularly good fit?
<--- Score

104. Should you invest in industry-recognized qualifications?
<--- Score

105. Is there an established change management process?
<--- Score

106. Were any designed experiments used to generate additional insight into the data analysis?
<--- Score

107. What are the processes for audit reporting and management?
<--- Score

108. What controls do you have in place to protect

data?
<--- Score

109. What is the cost of poor quality as supported by the team's analysis?
<--- Score

110. What are the necessary qualifications?
<--- Score

111. Have any additional benefits been identified that will result from closing all or most of the gaps?
<--- Score

112. A compounding model resolution with available relevant data can often provide insight towards a solution methodology; which privacy engineering models, tools and techniques are necessary?
<--- Score

113. Is there any way to speed up the process?
<--- Score

114. What qualifications do privacy engineering leaders need?
<--- Score

115. Have the problem and goal statements been updated to reflect the additional knowledge gained from the analyze phase?
<--- Score

116. Should the data subject be required to disclose real-world identity to access?
<--- Score

117. What qualifies as competition?
<--- Score

118. What are your outputs?
<--- Score

119. What privacy engineering metrics are outputs of the process?
<--- Score

120. What are your current levels and trends in key measures or indicators of privacy engineering product and process performance that are important to and directly serve your customers? How do these results compare with the performance of your competitors and other organizations with similar offerings?
<--- Score

121. What is your organizations system for selecting qualified vendors?
<--- Score

122. Is the gap/opportunity displayed and communicated in financial terms?
<--- Score

123. An organizationally feasible system request is one that considers the mission, goals and objectives of the organization, key questions are: is the privacy engineering solution request practical and will it solve a problem or take advantage of an opportunity to achieve company goals?
<--- Score

124. What are the privacy engineering design outputs?

<--- Score

125. How is data used for program management and improvement?
<--- Score

126. How do you define collaboration and team output?
<--- Score

127. What is your organizations process which leads to recognition of value generation?
<--- Score

128. Who owns what data?
<--- Score

129. What process improvements will be needed?
<--- Score

130. What methods do you use to gather privacy engineering data?
<--- Score

131. Do you understand your management processes today?
<--- Score

132. What were the financial benefits resulting from any 'ground fruit or low-hanging fruit' (quick fixes)?
<--- Score

133. Who is the data subject ?
<--- Score

134. What qualifications are needed?

<--- Score

135. Do your leaders quickly bounce back from setbacks?
<--- Score

136. How was the detailed process map generated, verified, and validated?
<--- Score

137. How can complex business processes cope with changes of the data in transit?
<--- Score

138. How often will data be collected for measures?
<--- Score

139. What systems/processes must you excel at?
<--- Score

140. Are you missing privacy engineering opportunities?
<--- Score

141. Do your employees have the opportunity to do what they do best everyday?
<--- Score

Add up total points for this section:
_____ = Total points for this section

Divided by: _____ (number of statements answered) = _____
Average score for this section

Transfer your score to the privacy

engineering Index at the beginning of
the Self-Assessment.

CRITERION #5: IMPROVE:

INTENT: Develop a practical solution. Innovate, establish and test the solution and to measure the results.

In my belief, the answer to this question is clearly defined:

5 Strongly Agree

4 Agree

3 Neutral

2 Disagree

1 Strongly Disagree

1. What assumptions are made about the solution and approach?
<--- Score

2. Do you cover the five essential competencies: Communication, Collaboration,Innovation, Adaptability, and Leadership that improve an organizations ability to leverage the new privacy engineering in a volatile global economy?

<--- Score

3. Do you combine technical expertise with business knowledge and privacy engineering Key topics include lifecycles, development approaches, requirements and how to make a business case?
<--- Score

4. Is the privacy engineering risk managed?
<--- Score

5. How scalable is your privacy engineering solution?
<--- Score

6. Who are the privacy engineering decision-makers?
<--- Score

7. What tools were used to evaluate the potential solutions?
<--- Score

8. How do you link measurement and risk?
<--- Score

9. How do you manage privacy engineering risk?
<--- Score

10. How do you improve productivity?
<--- Score

11. How does your organization evaluate strategic privacy engineering success?
<--- Score

12. Are the key business and technology risks being managed?

<--- Score

13. What tools were used to tap into the creativity and encourage 'outside the box' thinking?
<--- Score

14. How are policy decisions made and where?
<--- Score

15. How can you better manage risk?
<--- Score

16. What do you want to improve?
<--- Score

17. Would you develop a privacy engineering Communication Strategy?
<--- Score

18. What are the privacy engineering security risks?
<--- Score

19. What were the criteria for evaluating a privacy engineering pilot?
<--- Score

20. How do the privacy engineering results compare with the performance of your competitors and other organizations with similar offerings?
<--- Score

21. Have you identified breakpoints and/or risk tolerances that will trigger broad consideration of a potential need for intervention or modification of strategy?
<--- Score

22. What lessons, if any, from a pilot were incorporated into the design of the full-scale solution?
<--- Score

23. Who will be responsible for making the decisions to include or exclude requested changes once privacy engineering is underway?
<--- Score

24. Where do you need privacy engineering improvement?
<--- Score

25. What strategies for privacy engineering improvement are successful?
<--- Score

26. Which of the recognised risks out of all risks can be most likely transferred?
<--- Score

27. What are your current levels and trends in key measures or indicators of workforce and leader development?
<--- Score

28. What should a proof of concept or pilot accomplish?
<--- Score

29. What practices helps your organization to develop its capacity to recognize patterns?
<--- Score

30. Are risk management tasks balanced centrally and

locally?
<--- Score

31. Are decisions made in a timely manner?
<--- Score

32. privacy engineering risk decisions: whose call Is It?
<--- Score

33. How is knowledge sharing about risk
management improved?
<--- Score

34. What error proofing will be done to address some
of the discrepancies observed in the 'as is' process?
<--- Score

35. What tools were most useful during the improve
phase?
<--- Score

36. When you map the key players in your own work
and the types/domains of relationships with them,
which relationships do you find easy and which
challenging, and why?
<--- Score

37. Is any privacy engineering documentation
required?
<--- Score

38. What resources are required for the improvement
efforts?
<--- Score

39. Who manages supplier risk management in your

organization?
<--- Score

40. What went well, what should change, what can improve?
<--- Score

41. How will you measure the results?
<--- Score

42. Who do you report privacy engineering results to?
<--- Score

43. What is privacy engineering's impact on utilizing the best solution(s)?
<--- Score

44. Are procedures documented for managing privacy engineering risks?
<--- Score

45. How do you measure improved privacy engineering service perception, and satisfaction?
<--- Score

46. How is continuous improvement applied to risk management?
<--- Score

47. In the past few months, what is the smallest change you have made that has had the biggest positive result? What was it about that small change that produced the large return?
<--- Score

48. What are the implications of the one critical

privacy engineering decision 10 minutes, 10 months, and 10 years from now?
<--- Score

49. Risk Identification: What are the possible risk events your organization faces in relation to privacy engineering?
<--- Score

50. Explorations of the frontiers of privacy engineering will help you build influence, improve privacy engineering, optimize decision making, and sustain change, what is your approach?
<--- Score

51. What alternative responses are available to manage risk?
<--- Score

52. If you could go back in time five years, what decision would you make differently? What is your best guess as to what decision you're making today you might regret five years from now?
<--- Score

53. Are the most efficient solutions problem-specific?
<--- Score

54. Is the privacy engineering solution sustainable?
<--- Score

55. Is privacy engineering documentation maintained?
<--- Score

56. For decision problems, how do you develop a

decision statement?
<--- Score

57. How are privacy engineering risks managed?
<--- Score

58. How do you measure risk?
<--- Score

59. Is the privacy engineering documentation thorough?
<--- Score

60. Have you achieved privacy engineering improvements?
<--- Score

61. What is the magnitude of the improvements?
<--- Score

62. How do you manage and improve your privacy engineering work systems to deliver customer value and achieve organizational success and sustainability?
<--- Score

63. Who manages privacy engineering risk?
<--- Score

64. Who are the people involved in developing and implementing privacy engineering?
<--- Score

65. Is the solution technically practical?
<--- Score

66. What improvements have been achieved?

<--- Score

67. What are the affordable privacy engineering risks?
<--- Score

68. What to do with the results or outcomes of measurements?
<--- Score

69. Who makes the privacy engineering decisions in your organization?
<--- Score

70. Who are the key stakeholders for the privacy engineering evaluation?
<--- Score

71. What privacy engineering improvements can be made?
<--- Score

72. At what point will vulnerability assessments be performed once privacy engineering is put into production (e.g., ongoing Risk Management after implementation)?
<--- Score

73. Do those selected for the privacy engineering team have a good general understanding of what privacy engineering is all about?
<--- Score

74. Do vendor agreements bring new compliance risk ?
<--- Score

75. Can you identify any significant risks or exposures to privacy engineering third- parties (vendors, service providers, alliance partners etc) that concern you?
<--- Score

76. Are the risks fully understood, reasonable and manageable?
<--- Score

77. How do you improve privacy engineering service perception, and satisfaction?
<--- Score

78. What criteria will you use to assess your privacy engineering risks?
<--- Score

79. Which privacy engineering solution is appropriate?
<--- Score

80. Can the solution be designed and implemented within an acceptable time period?
<--- Score

81. How do you go about comparing privacy engineering approaches/solutions?
<--- Score

82. Who controls the risk?
<--- Score

83. How does the team improve its work?
<--- Score

84. How can the phases of privacy engineering

development be identified?
<--- Score

85. Is supporting privacy engineering documentation required?
<--- Score

86. How do you deal with privacy engineering risk?
<--- Score

87. What are the concrete privacy engineering results?
<--- Score

88. Where do the privacy engineering decisions reside?
<--- Score

89. What are the expected privacy engineering results?
<--- Score

90. Who are the privacy engineering decision makers?
<--- Score

91. Who will be responsible for documenting the privacy engineering requirements in detail?
<--- Score

92. What actually has to improve and by how much?
<--- Score

93. Why improve in the first place?
<--- Score

94. What were the underlying assumptions on the cost-benefit analysis?

<--- Score

95. How can you improve performance?
<--- Score

96. Who should make the privacy engineering decisions?
<--- Score

97. How risky is your organization?
<--- Score

98. For estimation problems, how do you develop an estimation statement?
<--- Score

99. What is privacy engineering risk?
<--- Score

100. How will you recognize and celebrate results?
<--- Score

101. Who controls key decisions that will be made?
<--- Score

102. Is there any other privacy engineering solution?
<--- Score

103. Is the measure of success for privacy engineering understandable to a variety of people?
<--- Score

104. What current systems have to be understood and/or changed?
<--- Score

105. How do you mitigate privacy engineering risk?
<--- Score

106. Do you need to do a usability evaluation?
<--- Score

107. How do you keep improving privacy engineering?
<--- Score

108. What risks do you need to manage?
<--- Score

109. Does a good decision guarantee a good outcome?
<--- Score

110. What is the team's contingency plan for potential problems occurring in implementation?
<--- Score

111. How do you define the solutions' scope?
<--- Score

112. To what extent does management recognize privacy engineering as a tool to increase the results?
<--- Score

113. How will you know that you have improved?
<--- Score

114. How do you improve your likelihood of success ?
<--- Score

115. Are risk triggers captured?
<--- Score

116. What can you do to improve?
<--- Score

117. How can skill-level changes improve privacy engineering?
<--- Score

118. What area needs the greatest improvement?
<--- Score

119. Who will be using the results of the measurement activities?
<--- Score

120. Is there a high likelihood that any recommendations will achieve their intended results?
<--- Score

121. How will you know when its improved?
<--- Score

122. Do you have the optimal project management team structure?
<--- Score

123. Can you integrate quality management and risk management?
<--- Score

124. Risk factors: what are the characteristics of privacy engineering that make it risky?
<--- Score

125. How significant is the improvement in the eyes of the end user?

<--- Score

126. Risk events: what are the things that could go wrong?
<--- Score

127. What is the implementation plan?
<--- Score

128. Is the scope clearly documented?
<--- Score

129. How will you know that a change is an improvement?
<--- Score

130. Are events managed to resolution?
<--- Score

131. What is the privacy engineering's sustainability risk?
<--- Score

132. Was a privacy engineering charter developed?
<--- Score

133. Will the controls trigger any other risks?
<--- Score

134. How can you improve privacy engineering?
<--- Score

135. Does the goal represent a desired result that can be measured?
<--- Score

Add up total points for this section:
_____ = Total points for this section

Divided by: _____ (number of
statements answered) = _____
Average score for this section

Transfer your score to the privacy
engineering Index at the beginning of
the Self-Assessment.

CRITERION #6: CONTROL:

INTENT: Implement the practical solution. Maintain the performance and correct possible complications.

In my belief, the answer to this question is clearly defined:

5 Strongly Agree

4 Agree

3 Neutral

2 Disagree

1 Strongly Disagree

1. How do you select, collect, align, and integrate privacy engineering data and information for tracking daily operations and overall organizational performance, including progress relative to strategic objectives and action plans?
<--- Score

2. How is privacy engineering project cost planned, managed, monitored?

<--- Score

3. Does the privacy engineering performance meet the customer's requirements?
<--- Score

4. Has the improved process and its steps been standardized?
<--- Score

5. Who will be in control?
<--- Score

6. What can you control?
<--- Score

7. You may have created your quality measures at a time when you lacked resources, technology wasn't up to the required standard, or low service levels were the industry norm. Have those circumstances changed?
<--- Score

8. How will privacy engineering decisions be made and monitored?
<--- Score

9. How will the process owner verify improvement in present and future sigma levels, process capabilities?
<--- Score

10. Is there a transfer of ownership and knowledge to process owner and process team tasked with the responsibilities.
<--- Score

11. Who sets the privacy engineering standards?
<--- Score

12. Do you monitor the effectiveness of your privacy engineering activities?
<--- Score

13. What is your plan to assess your security risks?
<--- Score

14. What adjustments to the strategies are needed?
<--- Score

15. How do you establish and deploy modified action plans if circumstances require a shift in plans and rapid execution of new plans?
<--- Score

16. Act/Adjust: What Do you Need to Do Differently?
<--- Score

17. What is the best design framework for privacy engineering organization now that, in a post industrial-age if the top-down, command and control model is no longer relevant?
<--- Score

18. Are operating procedures consistent?
<--- Score

19. Is knowledge gained on process shared and institutionalized?
<--- Score

20. Is there documentation that will support the successful operation of the improvement?

<--- Score

21. How do you plan on providing proper recognition
and disclosure of supporting companies?
<--- Score

22. What are customers monitoring?
<--- Score

23. How likely is the current privacy engineering plan
to come in on schedule or on budget?
<--- Score

24. What are the known security controls?
<--- Score

25. What should the next improvement project be
that is related to privacy engineering?
<--- Score

26. How can you best use all of your knowledge
repositories to enhance learning and sharing?
<--- Score

27. Are you measuring, monitoring and predicting
privacy engineering activities to optimize operations
and profitability, and enhancing outcomes?
<--- Score

28. Implementation Planning: is a pilot needed to test
the changes before a full roll out occurs?
<--- Score

29. Against what alternative is success being
measured?
<--- Score

30. How will the process owner and team be able to hold the gains?
<--- Score

31. How will the day-to-day responsibilities for monitoring and continual improvement be transferred from the improvement team to the process owner?
<--- Score

32. What are the key elements of your privacy engineering performance improvement system, including your evaluation, organizational learning, and innovation processes?
<--- Score

33. What are your results for key measures or indicators of the accomplishment of your privacy engineering strategy and action plans, including building and strengthening core competencies?
<--- Score

34. Is new knowledge gained imbedded in the response plan?
<--- Score

35. How do controls support value?
<--- Score

36. What privacy engineering standards are applicable?
<--- Score

37. How do you plan for the cost of succession?
<--- Score

38. What is the control/monitoring plan?
<--- Score

39. How widespread is its use?
<--- Score

40. Can you adapt and adjust to changing privacy engineering situations?
<--- Score

41. How do your controls stack up?
<--- Score

42. Is a response plan established and deployed?
<--- Score

43. Are the privacy engineering standards challenging?
<--- Score

44. Are the planned controls in place?
<--- Score

45. What key inputs and outputs are being measured on an ongoing basis?
<--- Score

46. Are suggested corrective/restorative actions indicated on the response plan for known causes to problems that might surface?
<--- Score

47. Have new or revised work instructions resulted?
<--- Score

48. Where do ideas that reach policy makers and planners as proposals for privacy engineering strengthening and reform actually originate?
<--- Score

49. Is there a standardized process?
<--- Score

50. How is change control managed?
<--- Score

51. How will you measure your QA plan's effectiveness?
<--- Score

52. Will your goals reflect your program budget?
<--- Score

53. What other systems, operations, processes, and infrastructures (hiring practices, staffing, training, incentives/rewards, metrics/dashboards/scorecards, etc.) need updates, additions, changes, or deletions in order to facilitate knowledge transfer and improvements?
<--- Score

54. Is a response plan in place for when the input, process, or output measures indicate an 'out-of-control' condition?
<--- Score

55. Does job training on the documented procedures need to be part of the process team's education and training?
<--- Score

56. Is there a recommended audit plan for routine surveillance inspections of privacy engineering's gains?
<--- Score

57. What is the recommended frequency of auditing?
<--- Score

58. Does privacy engineering appropriately measure and monitor risk?
<--- Score

59. What do you measure to verify effectiveness gains?
<--- Score

60. What are you attempting to measure/monitor?
<--- Score

61. What other areas of the group might benefit from the privacy engineering team's improvements, knowledge, and learning?
<--- Score

62. Is there an action plan in case of emergencies?
<--- Score

63. Is there a documented and implemented monitoring plan?
<--- Score

64. Are new process steps, standards, and documentation ingrained into normal operations?
<--- Score

65. Will any special training be provided for results

interpretation?
<--- Score

66. Are controls in place and consistently applied?
<--- Score

67. Is the privacy engineering test/monitoring cost justified?
<--- Score

68. How do you encourage people to take control and responsibility?
<--- Score

69. Who is going to spread your message?
<--- Score

70. How will report readings be checked to effectively monitor performance?
<--- Score

71. What should you measure to verify efficiency gains?
<--- Score

72. What do your reports reflect?
<--- Score

73. Do the privacy engineering decisions you make today help people and the planet tomorrow?
<--- Score

74. In the case of a privacy engineering project, the criteria for the audit derive from implementation objectives, an audit of a privacy engineering project involves assessing whether the recommendations

outlined for implementation have been met, can you track that any privacy engineering project is implemented as planned, and is it working?
<--- Score

75. Can support from partners be adjusted?
<--- Score

76. How might the group capture best practices and lessons learned so as to leverage improvements?
<--- Score

77. What are the critical parameters to watch?
<--- Score

78. Are documented procedures clear and easy to follow for the operators?
<--- Score

79. How do senior leaders actions reflect a commitment to the organizations privacy engineering values?
<--- Score

80. Does the response plan contain a definite closed loop continual improvement scheme (e.g., plan-do-check-act)?
<--- Score

81. How will new or emerging customer needs/requirements be checked/communicated to orient the process toward meeting the new specifications and continually reducing variation?
<--- Score

82. Is there a control plan in place for sustaining

improvements (short and long-term)?
<--- Score

83. What is the standard for acceptable privacy engineering performance?
<--- Score

84. Is reporting being used or needed?
<--- Score

85. What are the performance and scale of the privacy engineering tools?
<--- Score

86. Do you monitor the privacy engineering decisions made and fine tune them as they evolve?
<--- Score

87. How will input, process, and output variables be checked to detect for sub-optimal conditions?
<--- Score

88. Who is the privacy engineering process owner?
<--- Score

89. Who has control over resources?
<--- Score

90. Who controls critical resources?
<--- Score

91. Are there documented procedures?
<--- Score

92. Will the team be available to assist members in planning investigations?

<--- Score

93. What do you stand for--and what are you against?
<--- Score

94. How do you spread information?
<--- Score

95. Are pertinent alerts monitored, analyzed and distributed to appropriate personnel?
<--- Score

96. Do the viable solutions scale to future needs?
<--- Score

97. What quality tools were useful in the control phase?
<--- Score

98. Does a troubleshooting guide exist or is it needed?
<--- Score

99. Will existing staff require re-training, for example, to learn new business processes?
<--- Score

Add up total points for this section:
_ _ _ _ _ = Total points for this section

Divided by: _ _ _ _ _ _ (number of statements answered) = _ _ _ _ _ _
Average score for this section

Transfer your score to the privacy engineering Index at the beginning of the Self-Assessment.

CRITERION #7: SUSTAIN:

INTENT: Retain the benefits.

In my belief, the answer to this question is clearly defined:

5 Strongly Agree

4 Agree

3 Neutral

2 Disagree

1 Strongly Disagree

1. Which privacy engineering goals are the most important?
<--- Score

2. Do you think you know, or do you know you know ?
<--- Score

3. What are you trying to prove to yourself, and how might it be hijacking your life and business success?
<--- Score

4. Marketing budgets are tighter, consumers are more skeptical, and social media has changed forever the way we talk about privacy engineering, how do you gain traction?
<--- Score

5. Is there any existing privacy engineering governance structure?
<--- Score

6. How do you govern and fulfill your societal responsibilities?
<--- Score

7. Who do you think the world wants your organization to be?
<--- Score

8. How do you lead with privacy engineering in mind?
<--- Score

9. Who is responsible for privacy engineering?
<--- Score

10. Do you have past privacy engineering successes?
<--- Score

11. Would you rather sell to knowledgeable and informed customers or to uninformed customers?
<--- Score

12. If you do not follow, then how to lead?
<--- Score

13. Is your strategy driving your strategy? Or is the way in which you allocate resources driving your

strategy?
<--- Score

14. How do you transition from the baseline to the target?
<--- Score

15. How do you keep the momentum going?
<--- Score

16. What did you miss in the interview for the worst hire you ever made?
<--- Score

17. Can the schedule be done in the given time?
<--- Score

18. To whom do you add value?
<--- Score

19. What privacy engineering skills are most important?
<--- Score

20. What are the barriers to increased privacy engineering production?
<--- Score

21. Is it economical; do you have the time and money?
<--- Score

22. Will there be any necessary staff changes (redundancies or new hires)?
<--- Score

23. Ask yourself: how would you do this work if you

only had one staff member to do it?
<--- Score

24. Who have you, as a company, historically been when you've been at your best?
<--- Score

25. What are the business goals privacy engineering is aiming to achieve?
<--- Score

26. What counts that you are not counting?
<--- Score

27. What is the recommended frequency of auditing?
<--- Score

28. How do you manage privacy engineering Knowledge Management (KM)?
<--- Score

29. What relationships among privacy engineering trends do you perceive?
<--- Score

30. In retrospect, of the projects that you pulled the plug on, what percent do you wish had been allowed to keep going, and what percent do you wish had ended earlier?
<--- Score

31. If you find that you havent accomplished one of the goals for one of the steps of the privacy engineering strategy, what will you do to fix it?
<--- Score

32. Who uses your product in ways you never expected?
<--- Score

33. Instead of going to current contacts for new ideas, what if you reconnected with dormant contacts-- the people you used to know? If you were going reactivate a dormant tie, who would it be?
<--- Score

34. What are the long-term privacy engineering goals?
<--- Score

35. What happens at your organization when people fail?
<--- Score

36. How do you deal with privacy engineering changes?
<--- Score

37. What are the key enablers to make this privacy engineering move?
<--- Score

38. What is your formula for success in privacy engineering ?
<--- Score

39. What is your privacy engineering strategy?
<--- Score

40. In a project to restructure privacy engineering outcomes, which stakeholders would you involve?
<--- Score

41. Why do and why don't your customers like your organization?
<--- Score

42. How do you set privacy engineering stretch targets and how do you get people to not only participate in setting these stretch targets but also that they strive to achieve these?
<--- Score

43. Will it be accepted by users?
<--- Score

44. What tools do you use once you have decided on a privacy engineering strategy and more importantly how do you choose?
<--- Score

45. How will you ensure you get what you expected?
<--- Score

46. How do you determine the key elements that affect privacy engineering workforce satisfaction, how are these elements determined for different workforce groups and segments?
<--- Score

47. How important is privacy engineering to the user organizations mission?
<--- Score

48. How do you know if you are successful?
<--- Score

49. How do you proactively clarify deliverables and privacy engineering quality expectations?

<--- Score

50. How do you engage the workforce, in addition to satisfying them?
<--- Score

51. Is privacy engineering dependent on the successful delivery of a current project?
<--- Score

52. Who will provide the final approval of privacy engineering deliverables?
<--- Score

53. If you had to rebuild your organization without any traditional competitive advantages (i.e., no killer technology, promising research, innovative product/ service delivery model, etcetera), how would your people have to approach their work and collaborate together in order to create the necessary conditions for success?
<--- Score

54. How do you make it meaningful in connecting privacy engineering with what users do day-to-day?
<--- Score

55. Do you think privacy engineering accomplishes the goals you expect it to accomplish?
<--- Score

56. What projects are going on in the organization today, and what resources are those projects using from the resource pools?
<--- Score

57. How long will it take to change?
<--- Score

58. What are the short and long-term privacy engineering goals?
<--- Score

59. How do you go about securing privacy engineering?
<--- Score

60. What does your signature ensure?
<--- Score

61. What business benefits will privacy engineering goals deliver if achieved?
<--- Score

62. How will you insure seamless interoperability of privacy engineering moving forward?
<--- Score

63. How can you incorporate support to ensure safe and effective use of privacy engineering into the services that you provide?
<--- Score

64. Is the privacy engineering organization completing tasks effectively and efficiently?
<--- Score

65. What is the range of capabilities?
<--- Score

66. Who are your customers?
<--- Score

67. Who are the key stakeholders?
<--- Score

68. How do you accomplish your long range privacy engineering goals?
<--- Score

69. What unique value proposition (UVP) do you offer?
<--- Score

70. Are you / should you be revolutionary or evolutionary?
<--- Score

71. How do customers see your organization?
<--- Score

72. What are you challenging?
<--- Score

73. How do you listen to customers to obtain actionable information?
<--- Score

74. What is your BATNA (best alternative to a negotiated agreement)?
<--- Score

75. Why not do privacy engineering?
<--- Score

76. What information is critical to your organization that your executives are ignoring?
<--- Score

77. Who, on the executive team or the board, has spoken to a customer recently?
<--- Score

78. What is the overall talent health of your organization as a whole at senior levels, and for each organization reporting to a member of the Senior Leadership Team?
<--- Score

79. Why is privacy engineering important for you now?
<--- Score

80. Political -is anyone trying to undermine this project?
<--- Score

81. What goals did you miss?
<--- Score

82. What happens if you do not have enough funding?
<--- Score

83. Who will determine interim and final deadlines?
<--- Score

84. What trophy do you want on your mantle?
<--- Score

85. How do you create buy-in?
<--- Score

86. Where can you break convention?
<--- Score

87. How do you foster innovation?
<--- Score

88. Why is it important to have senior management support for a privacy engineering project?
<--- Score

89. At what moment would you think; Will I get fired?
<--- Score

90. What are strategies for increasing support and reducing opposition?
<--- Score

91. Why should people listen to you?
<--- Score

92. Are designers ready for privacy by design?
<--- Score

93. Can you do all this work?
<--- Score

94. What must you excel at?
<--- Score

95. How do you track customer value, profitability or financial return, organizational success, and sustainability?
<--- Score

96. What is the estimated value of the project?
<--- Score

97. What role does communication play in the success

or failure of a privacy engineering project?
<--- Score

98. What is an unauthorized commitment?
<--- Score

99. What you are going to do to affect the numbers?
<--- Score

100. Which models, tools and techniques are necessary?
<--- Score

101. What should you stop doing?
<--- Score

102. Can you maintain your growth without detracting from the factors that have contributed to your success?
<--- Score

103. What are specific privacy engineering rules to follow?
<--- Score

104. What was the last experiment you ran?
<--- Score

105. What are your most important goals for the strategic privacy engineering objectives?
<--- Score

106. What will be the consequences to the stakeholder (financial, reputation etc) if privacy engineering does not go ahead or fails to deliver the objectives?

<--- Score

107. What are the potential basics of privacy engineering fraud?
<--- Score

108. What new services of functionality will be implemented next with privacy engineering ?
<--- Score

109. Who do we want your customers to become?
<--- Score

110. Why will customers want to buy your organizations products/services?
<--- Score

111. What stupid rule would you most like to kill?
<--- Score

112. What would have to be true for the option on the table to be the best possible choice?
<--- Score

113. Is privacy engineering realistic, or are you setting yourself up for failure?
<--- Score

114. Whose voice (department, ethnic group, women, older workers, etc) might you have missed hearing from in your company, and how might you amplify this voice to create positive momentum for your business?
<--- Score

115. What trouble can you get into?

<--- Score

116. What is your competitive advantage?
<--- Score

117. Which functions and people interact with the supplier and or customer?
<--- Score

118. What is something you believe that nearly no one agrees with you on?
<--- Score

119. What management system can you use to leverage the privacy engineering experience, ideas, and concerns of the people closest to the work to be done?
<--- Score

120. Are the assumptions believable and achievable?
<--- Score

121. What is the overall business strategy?
<--- Score

122. What knowledge, skills and characteristics mark a good privacy engineering project manager?
<--- Score

123. Is maximizing privacy engineering protection the same as minimizing privacy engineering loss?
<--- Score

124. How will you motivate the stakeholders with the least vested interest?
<--- Score

125. What is a feasible sequencing of reform initiatives over time?

<--- Score

126. What are the success criteria that will indicate that privacy engineering objectives have been met and the benefits delivered?

<--- Score

127. What is your question? Why?

<--- Score

128. What privacy engineering modifications can you make work for you?

<--- Score

129. How do you ensure that implementations of privacy engineering products are done in a way that ensures safety?

<--- Score

130. What is the kind of project structure that would be appropriate for your privacy engineering project, should it be formal and complex, or can it be less formal and relatively simple?

<--- Score

131. Is there a work around that you can use?

<--- Score

132. How do you keep records, of what?

<--- Score

133. Which individuals, teams or departments will be involved in privacy engineering?

<--- Score

134. What is the craziest thing you can do?
<--- Score

135. What are the top 3 things at the forefront of your privacy engineering agendas for the next 3 years?
<--- Score

136. Who will be responsible for deciding whether privacy engineering goes ahead or not after the initial investigations?
<--- Score

137. Think of your privacy engineering project, what are the main functions?
<--- Score

138. What are internal and external privacy engineering relations?
<--- Score

139. Who else should you help?
<--- Score

140. Who do you want your customers to become?
<--- Score

141. What have you done to protect your business from competitive encroachment?
<--- Score

142. How do senior leaders deploy your organizations vision and values through your leadership system, to the workforce, to key suppliers and partners, and to customers and other stakeholders, as appropriate?

<--- Score

143. Who is responsible for errors?
<--- Score

144. When information truly is ubiquitous, when reach and connectivity are completely global, when computing resources are infinite, and when a whole new set of impossibilities are not only possible, but happening, what will that do to your business?
<--- Score

145. Is a privacy engineering team work effort in place?
<--- Score

146. How is implementation research currently incorporated into each of your goals?
<--- Score

147. Are you making progress, and are you making progress as privacy engineering leaders?
<--- Score

148. How do you provide a safe environment -physically and emotionally?
<--- Score

149. What could happen if you do not do it?
<--- Score

150. Who is responsible for ensuring appropriate resources (time, people and money) are allocated to privacy engineering?
<--- Score

151. What are the rules and assumptions your industry operates under? What if the opposite were true?
<--- Score

152. Operational - will it work?
<--- Score

153. What is the purpose of privacy engineering in relation to the mission?
<--- Score

154. Are the criteria for selecting recommendations stated?
<--- Score

155. Who are four people whose careers you have enhanced?
<--- Score

156. What are your personal philosophies regarding privacy engineering and how do they influence your work?
<--- Score

157. What are the challenges?
<--- Score

158. Is there any reason to believe the opposite of my current belief?
<--- Score

159. What may be the consequences for the performance of an organization if all stakeholders are not consulted regarding privacy engineering?
<--- Score

160. In the past year, what have you done (or could you have done) to increase the accurate perception of your company/brand as ethical and honest?
<--- Score

161. What would you recommend your friend do if he/she were facing this dilemma?
<--- Score

162. What have been your experiences in defining long range privacy engineering goals?
<--- Score

163. What is the funding source for this project?
<--- Score

164. What are the gaps in your knowledge and experience?
<--- Score

165. How will you know that the privacy engineering project has been successful?
<--- Score

166. How do you foster the skills, knowledge, talents, attributes, and characteristics you want to have?
<--- Score

167. What happens when a new employee joins the organization?
<--- Score

168. What one word do you want to own in the minds of your customers, employees, and partners?
<--- Score

Add up total points for this section:
_____ = Total points for this section

Divided by: _____ (number of
statements answered) = _____
Average score for this section

Transfer your score to the privacy
engineering Index at the beginning of
the Self-Assessment.

Privacy Engineering and Managing Projects, Criteria for Project Managers:

1.0 Initiating Process Group: Privacy Engineering

1. Based on your Privacy Engineering project communication management plan, what worked well?

2. At which stage, in a typical Privacy Engineering project do stake holders have maximum influence?

3. If action is called for, what form should it take?

4. How can you make your needs known?

5. How well defined and documented were the Privacy Engineering project management processes you chose to use?

6. Were decisions made in a timely manner?

7. Are you properly tracking the progress of the Privacy Engineering project and communicating the status to stakeholders?

8. Do you understand the communication expectations for this Privacy Engineering project?

9. What will you do?

10. What were things that you need to improve?

11. What communication items need improvement?

12. Do you know all the stakeholders impacted by the Privacy Engineering project and what needs are?

13. Who is performing the work of the Privacy Engineering project?

14. What do they need to know about the Privacy Engineering project?

15. Did the Privacy Engineering project team have the right skills?

16. Do you understand all business (operational), technical, resource and vendor risks associated with the Privacy Engineering project?

17. Contingency planning. if a risk event occurs, what will you do?

18. Who does what?

19. Measurable - are the targets measurable?

1.1 Project Charter: Privacy Engineering

20. Environmental stewardship and sustainability considerations: what is the process that will be used to ensure compliance with the environmental stewardship policy?

21. Why have you chosen the aim you have set forth?

22. Why do you need to manage scope?

23. Where and how does the team fit within your organization structure?

24. What outcome, in measureable terms, are you hoping to accomplish?

25. What is the purpose of the Privacy Engineering project?

26. What goes into your Privacy Engineering project Charter?

27. For whom?

28. What ideas do you have for initial tests of change (PDSA cycles)?

29. What barriers do you predict to your success?

30. Is it an improvement over existing products?

31. Are there special technology requirements?

32. Privacy Engineering project background: what is the primary motivation for this Privacy Engineering project?

33. Assumptions: what factors, for planning purposes, are you considering to be true?

34. Are you building in-house ?

35. Customer: who are you doing the Privacy Engineering project for?

36. When?

37. Dependent Privacy Engineering projects: what Privacy Engineering projects must be underway or completed before this Privacy Engineering project can be successful?

38. Strategic fit: what is the strategic initiative identifier for this Privacy Engineering project?

39. Where does all this information come from?

1.2 Stakeholder Register: Privacy Engineering

40. How should employers make voices heard?

41. Is your organization ready for change?

42. What is the power of the stakeholder?

43. How will reports be created?

44. What & Why?

45. Who wants to talk about Security?

46. Who is managing stakeholder engagement?

47. How big is the gap?

48. Who are the stakeholders?

49. How much influence do they have on the Privacy Engineering project?

50. What are the major Privacy Engineering project milestones requiring communications or providing communications opportunities?

51. What opportunities exist to provide communications?

1.3 Stakeholder Analysis Matrix: Privacy Engineering

52. Reliability of data, plan predictability?

53. What tools would help you communicate?

54. If the baseline is now, and if its improved it will be better than now?

55. What is the issue at stake?

56. Why do you care?

57. Are the required specifications for products or services changing?

58. Who will be affected by the Privacy Engineering project?

59. What is your Advocacy Strategy?

60. Who influences whom?

61. What is in it for you?

62. How will the stakeholder directly benefit from the Privacy Engineering project and how will this affect the stakeholders motivation?

63. Are there people who ise voices or interests in the issue may not be heard?

64. Has there been a similar initiative in the region?

65. Are they likely to influence the success or failure of your Privacy Engineering project?

66. How do they affect the Privacy Engineering project and its outcomes?

67. Competitor intentions - various?

68. Advantages of proposition?

69. New technologies, services, ideas?

70. Organizational Applicability?

71. Who is influential in the Privacy Engineering project area (both thematic and geographic areas)?

2.0 Planning Process Group: Privacy Engineering

72. If a task is partitionable, is this a sufficient condition to reduce the Privacy Engineering project duration?

73. Is the pace of implementing the products of the program ensuring the completeness of the results of the Privacy Engineering project?

74. How are the principles of aid effectiveness (ownership, alignment, management for development results and mutual responsibility) being applied in the Privacy Engineering project?

75. To what extent has the intervention strategy been adapted to the areas of intervention in which it is being implemented?

76. Is the duration of the program sufficient to ensure a cycle that will Privacy Engineering project the sustainability of the interventions?

77. Are the necessary foundations in place to ensure the sustainability of the results of the Privacy Engineering project?

78. Why is it important to determine activity sequencing on Privacy Engineering projects?

79. You did your readings, yes?

80. Have more efficient (sensitive) and appropriate measures been adopted to respond to the political and socio-cultural problems identified?

81. What is a Software Development Life Cycle (SDLC)?

82. Just how important is your work to the overall success of the Privacy Engineering project?

83. First of all, should any action be taken?

84. What good practices or successful experiences or transferable examples have been identified?

85. Is your organization showing technical capacity and leadership commitment to keep working with the Privacy Engineering project and to repeat it?

86. When will the Privacy Engineering project be done?

87. To what extent is the program helping to influence your organizations policy framework?

88. To what extent are the participating departments coordinating with each other?

89. How well defined and documented are the Privacy Engineering project management processes you chose to use?

2.1 Project Management Plan: Privacy Engineering

90. What would you do differently?

91. Is there anything you would now do differently on your Privacy Engineering project based on past experience?

92. Are there non-structural buyout or relocation recommendations?

93. Are there any scope changes proposed for a previously authorized Privacy Engineering project?

94. Are there any windfall benefits that would accrue to the Privacy Engineering project sponsor or other parties?

95. What would you do differently what did not work?

96. Are comparable cost estimates used for comparing, screening and selecting alternative plans, and has a reasonable cost estimate been developed for the recommended plan?

97. Is the appropriate plan selected based on your organizations objectives and evaluation criteria expressed in Principles and Guidelines policies?

98. Is the budget realistic?

99. What are the constraints?

100. Do there need to be organizational changes?

101. If the Privacy Engineering project management plan is a comprehensive document that guides you in Privacy Engineering project execution and control, then what should it NOT contain?

102. Why Change?

103. Are there any Client staffing expectations?

104. Are calculations and results of analyzes essentially correct?

105. What worked well?

106. Was the peer (technical) review of the cost estimates duly coordinated with the cost estimate center of expertise and addressed in the review documentation and certification?

107. What are the deliverables?

108. What data/reports/tools/etc. do program managers need?

109. What are the assigned resources?

2.2 Scope Management Plan: Privacy Engineering

110. Time estimation – how much time will be needed?

111. Have the personnel with the necessary skills and competence been identified and has agreement for participation in the Privacy Engineering project been reached with the appropriate management?

112. What happens if scope changes?

113. Have the scope, objectives, costs, benefits and impacts been communicated to all involved and/or impacted stakeholders and work groups?

114. How difficult will it be to do specific activities on this Privacy Engineering project?

115. Is the Privacy Engineering project status reviewed with the steering and executive teams at appropriate intervals?

116. Have Privacy Engineering project management standards and procedures been identified / established and documented?

117. Describe how the deliverables will be verified against the Privacy Engineering project scope. To whom will the deliverables be first presented for inspection and verification?

118. Where do scope processes fit in?

119. Is there a formal set of procedures supporting Issues Management?

120. Is the steering committee active in Privacy Engineering project oversight?

121. Have the procedures for identifying budget variances been followed?

122. How do you plan to control Scope Creep?

123. What do you need to do to accomplish the goal or goals?

124. Were Privacy Engineering project team members involved in the development of activity & task decomposition?

125. Does the detailed work plan match the complexity of tasks with the capabilities of personnel?

126. Does a documented Privacy Engineering project organizational policy & plan (i.e. governance model) exist?

127. What are the risks that could significantly affect the scope of the Privacy Engineering project?

128. Is there a set of procedures defining the scope, procedures, and deliverables defining quality control?

129. Has the selected plan been formulated using cost effectiveness and incremental analysis techniques?

2.3 Requirements Management Plan: Privacy Engineering

130. What cost metrics will be used?

131. What is a problem?

132. Do you have an agreed upon process for alerting the Privacy Engineering project Manager if a request for change in requirements leads to a product scope change?

133. Will you have access to stakeholders when you need them?

134. Why manage requirements?

135. Is any organizational data being used or stored?

136. Will you perform a Requirements Risk assessment and develop a plan to deal with risks?

137. Are all the stakeholders ready for the transition into the user community?

138. How will the information be distributed?

139. Subject to change control?

140. Did you get proper approvals?

141. Will you document changes to requirements?

142. Could inaccurate or incomplete requirements in this Privacy Engineering project create a serious risk for the business?

143. Is the user satisfied?

144. How detailed should the Privacy Engineering project get?

145. Did you use declarative statements?

146. How often will the reporting occur?

147. Is the system software (non-operating system) new to the IT Privacy Engineering project team?

148. How will you develop the schedule of requirements activities?

149. How will unresolved questions be handled once approval has been obtained?

2.4 Requirements Documentation: Privacy Engineering

150. Has requirements gathering uncovered information that would necessitate changes?

151. How to document system requirements?

152. Consistency. are there any requirements conflicts?

153. Are there legal issues?

154. How does the proposed Privacy Engineering project contribute to the overall objectives of your organization?

155. Do technical resources exist?

156. Who provides requirements?

157. What images does it conjure?

158. Does your organization restrict technical alternatives?

159. How will the proposed Privacy Engineering project help?

160. The problem with gathering requirements is right there in the word gathering. What images does it conjure?

161. What are the acceptance criteria?

162. Have the benefits identified with the system being identified clearly?

163. Is the requirement properly understood?

164. What will be the integration problems?

165. How do you know when a Requirement is accurate enough?

166. What can tools do for us?

167. Who is interacting with the system?

168. What are the attributes of a customer?

169. Is the origin of the requirement clearly stated?

2.5 Requirements Traceability Matrix: Privacy Engineering

170. How small is small enough?

171. What percentage of Privacy Engineering projects are producing traceability matrices between requirements and other work products?

172. Will you use a Requirements Traceability Matrix?

173. Describe the process for approving requirements so they can be added to the traceability matrix and Privacy Engineering project work can be performed. Will the Privacy Engineering project requirements become approved in writing?

174. What is the WBS?

175. Why use a WBS?

176. Why do you manage scope?

177. How do you manage scope?

178. How will it affect the stakeholders personally in career?

179. What are the chronologies, contingencies, consequences, criteria?

180. Is there a requirements traceability process in place?

181. Do you have a clear understanding of all subcontracts in place?

2.6 Project Scope Statement: Privacy Engineering

182. What are the possible consequences should a risk come to occur?

183. Are there adequate Privacy Engineering project control systems?

184. Elements that deal with providing the detail?

185. Does the scope statement still need some clarity?

186. Is an issue management process documented and filed?

187. What actions will be taken to mitigate the risk?

188. Have the configuration management functions been assigned?

189. What is a process you might recommend to verify the accuracy of the research deliverable?

190. Were potential customers involved early in the planning process?

191. Is there an information system for the Privacy Engineering project?

192. Are the input requirements from the team members clearly documented and communicated?

193. Is the Privacy Engineering project sponsor function identified and defined?

194. Is your organization structure appropriate for the Privacy Engineering projects size and complexity?

195. Are there specific processes you will use to evaluate and approve/reject changes?

196. Will you need a statement of work?

197. Will the risk plan be updated on a regular and frequent basis?

198. If there are vendors, have they signed off on the Privacy Engineering project Plan?

199. Will this process be communicated to the customer and Privacy Engineering project team?

200. Do you anticipate new stakeholders joining the Privacy Engineering project over time?

201. Will the Privacy Engineering project risks be managed according to the Privacy Engineering projects risk management process?

2.7 Assumption and Constraint Log: Privacy Engineering

202. Are processes for release management of new development from coding and unit testing, to integration testing, to training, and production defined and followed?

203. What if failure during recovery?

204. No superfluous information or marketing narrative?

205. What is positive about the current process?

206. What other teams / processes would be impacted by changes to the current process, and how?

207. Do you know what your customers expectations are regarding this process?

208. How are new requirements or changes to requirements identified?

209. If it is out of compliance, should the process be amended or should the Plan be amended?

210. What to do at recovery?

211. Does the traceability documentation describe the tool and/or mechanism to be used to capture traceability throughout the life cycle?

212. What do you log?

213. Does the plan conform to standards?

214. Can the requirements be traced to the appropriate components of the solution, as well as test scripts?

215. Can you perform this task or activity in a more effective manner?

216. Security analysis has access to information that is sanitized?

217. What would you gain if you spent time working to improve this process?

218. Do the requirements meet the standards of correctness, completeness, consistency, accuracy, and readability?

219. Are there nonconformance issues?

2.8 Work Breakdown Structure: Privacy Engineering

220. Why would you develop a Work Breakdown Structure?

221. Who has to do it?

222. How many levels?

223. What has to be done?

224. Is it a change in scope?

225. Is it still viable?

226. Where does it take place?

227. What is the probability that the Privacy Engineering project duration will exceed xx weeks?

228. When does it have to be done?

229. How far down?

230. When would you develop a Work Breakdown Structure?

231. Is the work breakdown structure (wbs) defined and is the scope of the Privacy Engineering project clear with assigned deliverable owners?

232. What is the probability of completing the Privacy

Engineering project in less that xx days?

233. When do you stop?

234. Can you make it?

235. How will you and your Privacy Engineering project team define the Privacy Engineering projects scope and work breakdown structure?

236. How much detail?

237. How big is a work-package?

2.9 WBS Dictionary: Privacy Engineering

238. Is the work done on a work package level as described in the WBS dictionary?

239. Evaluate the performance of operating organizations?

240. Budgeted cost for work performed?

241. Are estimates developed by Privacy Engineering project personnel coordinated with the already stated responsible for overall management to determine whether required resources will be available according to revised planning?

242. Does the contractors system provide for accurate cost accumulation and assignment to control accounts in a manner consistent with the budgets using recognized acceptable costing techniques?

243. Does the contractors system include procedures for measuring the performance of critical subcontractors?

244. Are data elements (BCWS, BCWP, and ACWP) progressively summarized from the detail level to the contract level through the CWBS?

245. Detailed schedules which support control account and work package start and completion dates/events?

246. Is the entire contract planned in time-phased control accounts to the extent practicable?

247. What is the end result of a work package?

248. Is each control account assigned to a single organizational element directly responsible for the work and identifiable to a single element of the CWBS?

249. Are records maintained to show full accountability for all material purchased for the contract, including the residual inventory?

250. Do the lines of authority for incurring indirect costs correspond to the lines of responsibility for management control of the same components of costs?

251. Are retroactive changes to direct costs and indirect costs prohibited except for the correction of errors and routine accounting adjustments?

252. Is work properly classified as measured effort, LOE, or apportioned effort and appropriately separated?

253. Contractor financial periods; for example, annual?

254. Are the responsibilities and authorities of each of the above organizational elements or managers clearly defined?

255. Are estimates of costs at completion generated

in a rational, consistent manner?

256. Authorization to proceed with all authorized work?

2.10 Schedule Management Plan: Privacy Engineering

257. What does a valid Schedule look like?

258. Quality assurance overheads?

259. Goal: is the schedule feasible and at what cost?

260. List all schedule constraints here. Must the Privacy Engineering project be complete by a specified date?

261. Is documentation created for communication with the suppliers and Vendors?

262. Are the appropriate IT resources adequate to meet planned commitments?

263. Does the ims include all contract and/or designated management control milestones?

264. Were Privacy Engineering project team members involved in the development of activity & task decomposition?

265. Have all unresolved risks been documented?

266. Does the Privacy Engineering project have a formal Privacy Engineering project Charter?

267. Have adequate resources been provided by management to ensure Privacy Engineering project

success?

268. Are all key components of a Quality Assurance Plan present?

269. Are action items captured and managed?

270. Were stakeholders aware and supportive of the principles and practices of modern software estimation?

271. Have the key functions and capabilities been defined and assigned to each release or iteration?

272. Have all necessary approvals been obtained?

273. Are risk oriented checklists used during risk identification?

274. Pareto diagrams, statistical sampling, flow charting or trend analysis used quality monitoring?

275. Does a documented Privacy Engineering project organizational policy & plan (i.e. governance model) exist?

276. Has a provision been made to reassess Privacy Engineering project risks at various Privacy Engineering project stages?

2.11 Activity List: Privacy Engineering

277. How can the Privacy Engineering project be displayed graphically to better visualize the activities?

278. How much slack is available in the Privacy Engineering project?

279. What did not go as well?

280. How will it be performed?

281. What is your organizations history in doing similar activities?

282. How should ongoing costs be monitored to try to keep the Privacy Engineering project within budget?

283. What is the total time required to complete the Privacy Engineering project if no delays occur?

284. What went right?

285. Can you determine the activity that must finish, before this activity can start?

286. For other activities, how much delay can be tolerated?

287. The wbs is developed as part of a joint planning session. and how do you know that youhave done this right?

288. Who will perform the work?

289. Should you include sub-activities?

290. How difficult will it be to do specific activities on this Privacy Engineering project?

291. What is the LF and LS for each activity?

292. What will be performed?

293. Where will it be performed?

294. When do the individual activities need to start and finish?

295. What are you counting on?

296. What is the probability the Privacy Engineering project can be completed in xx weeks?

2.12 Activity Attributes: Privacy Engineering

297. Is there anything planned that does not need to be here?

298. Have constraints been applied to the start and finish milestones for the phases?

299. How do you manage time?

300. What is missing?

301. Resource is assigned to?

302. Activity: what is Missing?

303. Can you re-assign any activities to another resource to resolve an over-allocation?

304. How difficult will it be to complete specific activities on this Privacy Engineering project?

305. Have you identified the Activity Leveling Priority code value on each activity?

306. Do you feel very comfortable with your prediction?

307. Activity: what is In the Bag?

308. Which method produces the more accurate cost assignment?

309. How else could the items be grouped?

310. Were there other ways you could have organized the data to achieve similar results?

311. Is there a trend during the year?

312. What went wrong?

313. What activity do you think you should spend the most time on?

314. How difficult will it be to do specific activities on this Privacy Engineering project?

315. Can more resources be added?

316. How many resources do you need to complete the work scope within a limit of X number of days?

2.13 Milestone List: Privacy Engineering

317. Can you derive how soon can the whole Privacy Engineering project finish?

318. Calculate how long can activity be delayed?

319. Are the required resources available or need to be acquired?

320. Timescales, deadlines and pressures?

321. Political effects?

322. Information and research?

323. Identify critical paths (one or more) and which activities are on the critical path?

324. How soon can the activity start?

325. Sustainable financial backing?

326. When will the Privacy Engineering project be complete?

327. What is the market for your technology, product or service?

328. Milestone pages should display the UserID of the person who added the milestone. Does a report or query exist that provides this audit information?

329. Sustaining internal capabilities?

330. Describe your organizations strengths and core competencies. What factors will make your organization succeed?

331. Own known vulnerabilities?

332. Loss of key staff?

333. Level of the Innovation?

334. Marketing - reach, distribution, awareness?

335. Legislative effects?

336. How will the milestone be verified?

2.14 Network Diagram: Privacy Engineering

337. If x is long, what would be the completion time if you break x into two parallel parts of y weeks and z weeks?

338. What activities must follow this activity?

339. What is the completion time?

340. What controls the start and finish of a job?

341. Will crashing x weeks return more in benefits than it costs?

342. What job or jobs precede it?

343. Are the gantt chart and/or network diagram updated periodically and used to assess the overall Privacy Engineering project timetable?

344. Where do schedules come from?

345. What is the lowest cost to complete this Privacy Engineering project in xx weeks?

346. What job or jobs follow it?

347. Which type of network diagram allows you to depict four types of dependencies?

348. What are the Major Administrative Issues?

349. What is the probability of completing the Privacy Engineering project in less that xx days?

350. What must be completed before an activity can be started?

351. Where do you schedule uncertainty time?

352. How confident can you be in your milestone dates and the delivery date?

353. Exercise: what is the probability that the Privacy Engineering project duration will exceed xx weeks?

354. What job or jobs could run concurrently?

355. What are the Key Success Factors?

356. Review the logical flow of the network diagram. Take a look at which activities you have first and then sequence the activities. Do they make sense?

2.15 Activity Resource Requirements: Privacy Engineering

357. Anything else?

358. Are there unresolved issues that need to be addressed?

359. How many signatures do you require on a check and does this match what is in your policy and procedures?

360. What is the Work Plan Standard?

361. Time for overtime?

362. How do you handle petty cash?

363. When does monitoring begin?

364. Which logical relationship does the PDM use most often?

365. Why do you do that?

366. What are constraints that you might find during the Human Resource Planning process?

367. Do you use tools like decomposition and rolling-wave planning to produce the activity list and other outputs?

368. Other support in specific areas?

2.16 Resource Breakdown Structure: Privacy Engineering

369. What can you do to improve productivity?

370. Changes based on input from stakeholders?

371. Goals for the Privacy Engineering project. What is each stakeholders desired outcome for the Privacy Engineering project?

372. Why time management?

373. Is predictive resource analysis being done?

374. Who is allowed to see what data about which resources?

375. Who will be used as a Privacy Engineering project team member?

376. How difficult will it be to do specific activities on this Privacy Engineering project?

377. How should the information be delivered?

378. Any changes from stakeholders?

379. What is Privacy Engineering project communication management?

380. Are the required resources available?

381. Who needs what information?

382. Which resource planning tool provides information on resource responsibility and accountability?

383. What are the requirements for resource data?

384. Why do you do it?

385. What is the primary purpose of the human resource plan?

2.17 Activity Duration Estimates: Privacy Engineering

386. Is corrective action taken to bring Privacy Engineering project performance into line with the Privacy Engineering project plan?

387. How do functionality, system outputs, performance, reliability, and maintainability requirements affect quality planning?

388. Are Privacy Engineering project activities decomposed into manageable components to ensure expected management control?

389. What Privacy Engineering project was the first to use modern Privacy Engineering project management?

390. What is the BEST thing to do?

391. How does Privacy Engineering project management relate to other disciplines?

392. Why is there a new or renewed interest in the field of Privacy Engineering project management?

393. When a risk event occurs, is the risk response evaluated and the appropriate response implemented?

394. What is the critical path for this Privacy Engineering project and how long is it?

395. How does Privacy Engineering project integration management relate to the Privacy Engineering project life cycle, stakeholders, and the other Privacy Engineering project management knowledge areas?

396. Do you think many information technology professionals have experience writing RFPs and evaluating proposals for information technology Privacy Engineering projects?

397. Consider the common sources of risk on information technology Privacy Engineering projects and suggestions for managing them. Which suggestions do you find most useful?

398. What are the Privacy Engineering project management deliverables of each process group?

399. What is the duration of a milestone?

400. Will the new application be developed using existing hardware, software, and networks?

401. Which best describes how this affects the Privacy Engineering project?

402. Mass, power, cost ... why not time?

403. Is a standard form used to obtain bids and proposals from prospective sellers?

404. What is earned value?

2.18 Duration Estimating Worksheet: Privacy Engineering

405. Value pocket identification & quantification what are value pockets?

406. Is a construction detail attached (to aid in explanation)?

407. Why estimate costs?

408. Can the Privacy Engineering project be constructed as planned?

409. What is an Average Privacy Engineering project?

410. What questions do you have?

411. What info is needed?

412. What are the critical bottleneck activities?

413. How can the Privacy Engineering project be displayed graphically to better visualize the activities?

414. When does your organization expect to be able to complete it?

415. Will the Privacy Engineering project collaborate with the local community and leverage resources?

416. Science = process: remember the scientific method?

417. When, then?

418. Does the Privacy Engineering project provide innovative ways for stakeholders to overcome obstacles or deliver better outcomes?

419. What is next?

420. What is the total time required to complete the Privacy Engineering project if no delays occur?

421. How should ongoing costs be monitored to try to keep the Privacy Engineering project within budget?

2.19 Project Schedule: Privacy Engineering

422. Does the condition or event threaten the Privacy Engineering projects objectives in any ways?

423. Are key risk mitigation strategies added to the Privacy Engineering project schedule?

424. Have all Privacy Engineering project delays been adequately accounted for, communicated to all stakeholders and adjustments made in overall Privacy Engineering project schedule?

425. Is infrastructure setup part of your Privacy Engineering project?

426. Privacy Engineering project work estimates Who is managing the work estimate quality of work tasks in the Privacy Engineering project schedule?

427. Are you working on the right risks?

428. Are procedures defined by which the Privacy Engineering project schedule may be changed?

429. Why do you need schedules?

430. How effectively were issues able to be resolved without impacting the Privacy Engineering project Schedule or Budget?

431. Did the Privacy Engineering project come in

under budget?

432. What is risk?

433. What documents, if any, will the subcontractor provide (eg Privacy Engineering project schedule, quality plan etc)?

434. What is the purpose of a Privacy Engineering project schedule?

435. What does that mean?

436. What is Privacy Engineering project management?

437. Are activities connected because logic dictates the order in which others occur?

2.20 Cost Management Plan: Privacy Engineering

438. Are milestone deliverables effectively tracked and compared to Privacy Engineering project plan?

439. Are status reports received per the Privacy Engineering project Plan?

440. Cost estimate preparation – What cost estimates will be prepared during the Privacy Engineering project phases?

441. Is there anything unique in this Privacy Engineering projects scope statement that will affect resources?

442. Does the Privacy Engineering project have a Statement of Work?

443. Are the results of quality assurance reviews provided to affected groups & individuals?

444. Are mitigation strategies identified?

445. Progress measurement and control – How will the Privacy Engineering project measure and control progress?

446. Milestones – what are the key dates in executing the contract plan?

447. Have Privacy Engineering project team

accountabilities & responsibilities been clearly defined?

448. Are actuals compared against estimates to analyze and correct variances?

449. What would the life cycle costs be?

450. Has the Privacy Engineering project manager been identified?

451. What strengths do you have?

452. Are meeting objectives identified for each meeting?

453. Were Privacy Engineering project team members involved in the development of activity & task decomposition?

454. Are multiple estimation methods being employed?

455. Scope of work – What is the likelihood and extent of potential future changes to the Privacy Engineering project scope?

456. Are schedule deliverables actually delivered?

2.21 Activity Cost Estimates: Privacy Engineering

457. How do you change activities?

458. What is the activity inventory?

459. Were the tasks or work products prepared by the consultant useful?

460. Does the estimator have experience?

461. Based on your Privacy Engineering project communication management plan, what worked well?

462. How do you allocate indirect costs to activities?

463. When do you enter into PPM?

464. Will you use any tools, such as Privacy Engineering project management software, to assist in capturing Earned Value metrics?

465. Did the Privacy Engineering project team have the right skills?

466. Was the consultant knowledgeable about the program?

467. Certification of actual expenditures?

468. Scope statement only direct or indirect costs as

well?

469. Can you delete activities or make them inactive?

470. What skill level is required to do the job?

471. How many activities should you have?

472. Is costing method consistent with study goals?

2.22 Cost Estimating Worksheet: Privacy Engineering

473. Will the Privacy Engineering project collaborate with the local community and leverage resources?

474. Can a trend be established from historical performance data on the selected measure and are the criteria for using trend analysis or forecasting methods met?

475. Is the Privacy Engineering project responsive to community need?

476. What is the estimated labor cost today based upon this information?

477. How will the results be shared and to whom?

478. What costs are to be estimated?

479. What happens to any remaining funds not used?

480. Is it feasible to establish a control group arrangement?

481. What can be included?

482. Who is best positioned to know and assist in identifying corresponding factors?

483. Identify the timeframe necessary to monitor progress and collect data to determine how the

selected measure has changed?

484. What is the purpose of estimating?

485. What will others want?

486. Does the Privacy Engineering project provide innovative ways for stakeholders to overcome obstacles or deliver better outcomes?

487. Ask: are others positioned to know, are others credible, and will others cooperate?

488. What additional Privacy Engineering project(s) could be initiated as a result of this Privacy Engineering project?

2.23 Cost Baseline: Privacy Engineering

489. Definition of done can be traced back to the definitions of what are you providing to the customer in terms of deliverables?

490. Review your risk triggers -have your risks changed?

491. Have all approved changes to the schedule baseline been identified and impact on the Privacy Engineering project documented?

492. Have the lessons learned been filed with the Privacy Engineering project Management Office?

493. What is it ?

494. Is the requested change request a result of changes in other Privacy Engineering project(s)?

495. Does a process exist for establishing a cost baseline to measure Privacy Engineering project performance?

496. Who will use corresponding metrics ?

497. How accurate do cost estimates need to be?

498. Has the documentation relating to operation and maintenance of the product(s) or service(s) been delivered to, and accepted by, operations

management?

499. On budget?

500. Why do you manage cost?

501. How fast?

502. What is the reality?

503. What can go wrong?

504. Has the Privacy Engineering project (or Privacy Engineering project phase) been evaluated against each objective established in the product description and Integrated Privacy Engineering project Plan?

505. How concrete were original objectives?

506. Should a more thorough impact analysis be conducted?

2.24 Quality Management Plan: Privacy Engineering

507. Results Available?

508. How are data handled when a test is not run per specification?

509. How does your organization use comparative data and information to improve organizational performance?

510. How is equipment calibrated?

511. What process do you use to minimize errors, defects, and rework?

512. What is the return on investment?

513. How are deviations from procedures handled?

514. Who is responsible for writing the qapp?

515. Have you eliminated all duplicative tasks or manual efforts, where appropriate?

516. Do the data quality objectives communicate the intended program need?

517. What procedures are used to determine if you use, and the number of split, replicate or duplicate samples taken at a site?

518. Are there procedures in place to effectively manage interdependencies with other Privacy Engineering projects / systems?

519. How does your organization recruit, hire, and retain new employees?

520. Were there any deficiencies / issues in prior years self-assessment?

521. Are you meeting the quality standards?

522. Are there trends or hot spots?

523. Written by multiple authors and in multiple writing styles?

524. Documented results available?

525. How does your organization establish and maintain customer relationships?

2.25 Quality Metrics: Privacy Engineering

526. Where is quality now?

527. How can the effectiveness of each of the activities be measured?

528. How do you know if everyone is trying to improve the right things?

529. Which are the right metrics to use?

530. Are quality metrics defined?

531. Was material distributed on time?

532. What forces exist that would cause them to change?

533. What percentage are outcome-based?

534. Did evaluation start on time?

535. What documentation is required?

536. Is quality culture a competitive advantage?

537. What metrics are important and most beneficial to measure?

538. Should a modifier be included?

539. How do you calculate corresponding metrics?

540. Was review conducted per standard protocols?

541. Is there a set of procedures to capture, analyze and act on quality metrics?

542. What if the biggest risk to your business were the already stated people who do not complain?

543. The metrics—what is being considered?

544. Can you correlate your quality metrics to profitability?

545. Has it met internal or external standards?

2.26 Process Improvement Plan: Privacy Engineering

546. Where do you want to be?

547. What personnel are the coaches for your initiative?

548. How do you measure?

549. The motive is determined by asking, Why do you want to achieve this goal?

550. Purpose of goal: the motive is determined by asking, why do you want to achieve this goal?

551. Modeling current processes is great, and will you ever see a return on that investment?

552. Why do you want to achieve the goal?

553. What is quality and how will you ensure it?

554. Where do you focus?

555. Why quality management?

556. What personnel are the champions for the initiative?

557. What is the test-cycle concept?

558. Everyone agrees on what process improvement

is, right?

559. What lessons have you learned so far?

560. Have storage and access mechanisms and procedures been determined?

561. Does your process ensure quality?

562. Are you following the quality standards?

563. What personnel are the change agents for your initiative?

2.27 Responsibility Assignment Matrix: Privacy Engineering

564. Does a missing responsibility indicate that the current Privacy Engineering project is not yet fully understood?

565. Changes in the direct base to which overhead costs are allocated?

566. Does the accounting system provide a basis for auditing records of direct costs chargeable to the contract?

567. Who is responsible for work and budgets for each wbs?

568. Are people afraid to let you know when others are under allocated?

569. Competencies and craftsmanship – what competencies are necessary and what level?

570. Are your organizations and items of cost assigned to each pool identified?

571. Ideas for developing soft skills at your organization?

572. Changes in the current direct and Privacy Engineering projected base?

573. How do you assist them to be as productive as

possible?

574. Does the contractor use objective results, design reviews, and tests to trace schedule?

575. Undistributed budgets, if any?

576. Does the contractors system provide unit or lot costs when applicable?

577. Too many as: does a proper segregation of duties exist?

578. The anticipated business volume?

579. When performing is split among two or more roles, is the work clearly defined so that the efforts are coordinated and the communication is clear?

580. What do you need to implement earned value management?

581. Do you need to convince people that its well worth the time and effort?

2.28 Roles and Responsibilities: Privacy Engineering

582. To decide whether to use a quality measurement, ask how will you know when it is achieved?

583. Required skills, knowledge, experience?

584. Does the team have access to and ability to use data analysis tools?

585. Who is responsible for implementation activities and where will the functions, roles and responsibilities be defined?

586. What is working well?

587. Implementation of actions: Who are the responsible units?

588. Authority: what areas/Privacy Engineering projects in your work do you have the authority to decide upon and act on the already stated decisions?

589. Be specific; avoid generalities. Thank you and great work alone are insufficient. What exactly do you appreciate and why?

590. Who: who is involved?

591. Do the values and practices inherent in the culture of your organization foster or hinder the process?

592. Are your budgets supportive of a culture of quality data?

593. Does your vision/mission support a culture of quality data?

594. Attainable / achievable: the goal is attainable; can you actually accomplish the goal?

595. Was the expectation clearly communicated?

596. What areas would you highlight for changes or improvements?

597. Do you take the time to clearly define roles and responsibilities on Privacy Engineering project tasks?

598. Are governance roles and responsibilities documented?

599. What expectations were NOT met?

2.29 Human Resource Management Plan: Privacy Engineering

600. Were sponsors and decision makers available when needed outside regularly scheduled meetings?

601. Has a capability assessment been conducted?

602. Do Privacy Engineering project teams & team members report on status / activities / progress?

603. Are staff skills known and available for each task?

604. Who will be impacted (both positively and negatively) as a result of or during the execution of this Privacy Engineering project?

605. Do Privacy Engineering project managers participating in the Privacy Engineering project know the Privacy Engineering projects true status first hand?

606. Has a provision been made to reassess Privacy Engineering project risks at various Privacy Engineering project stages?

607. How to convince to employees that it is a necessary process?

608. Are risk triggers captured?

609. Where is your organization headed?

610. Is the communication plan being followed?

611. Have stakeholder accountabilities & responsibilities been clearly defined?

612. Are all vendor contracts closed out?

613. Are vendor invoices audited for accuracy before payment?

614. Are status reports received per the Privacy Engineering project Plan?

615. How well does your organization communicate?

2.30 Communications Management Plan: Privacy Engineering

616. Are others part of the communications management plan?

617. How will the person responsible for executing the communication item be notified?

618. Timing: when do the effects of the communication take place?

619. Who is the stakeholder?

620. Do you then often overlook a key stakeholder or stakeholder group?

621. Which stakeholders are thought leaders, influences, or early adopters?

622. How did the term stakeholder originate?

623. Who needs to know and how much?

624. In your work, how much time is spent on stakeholder identification?

625. Do you ask; can you recommend others for you to talk with about this initiative?

626. Who have you worked with in past, similar initiatives?

627. Is there an important stakeholder who is actively opposed and will not receive messages?

628. What is Privacy Engineering project communications management?

629. Are there too many who have an interest in some aspect of your work?

630. What is the stakeholders level of authority?

631. What to know?

632. Conflict resolution -which method when?

633. Are others needed?

634. What does the stakeholder need from the team?

2.31 Risk Management Plan: Privacy Engineering

635. Is Privacy Engineering project scope stable?

636. Mitigation -how can you avoid the risk?

637. Why do you want risk management?

638. What things might go wrong?

639. Should the risk be taken at all?

640. What is the impact to the Privacy Engineering project if the item is not resolved in a timely fashion?

641. Are the software tools integrated with each other?

642. How risk averse are you?

643. Are tools for analysis and design available?

644. Which risks should get the attention?

645. Have top software and customer managers formally committed to support the Privacy Engineering project?

646. Are there new risks that mitigation strategies might introduce?

647. Can the risk be avoided by choosing a different

alternative?

648. Technology risk: is the Privacy Engineering project technically feasible?

649. Is the process being followed?

650. Are the metrics meaningful and useful?

651. Is the process supported by tools?

652. Is the customer willing to participate in reviews?

653. Market risk: will the new product be useful to your organization or marketable to others?

654. How is risk monitoring performed?

2.32 Risk Register: Privacy Engineering

655. Financial risk -can your organization afford to undertake the Privacy Engineering project?

656. Are there any knock-on effects/impact on any of the other areas?

657. Market risk -will the new service or product be useful to your organization or marketable to others?

658. What evidence do you have to justify the likelihood score of the risk (audit, incident report, claim, complaints, inspection, internal review)?

659. What are the main aims, objectives of the policy, strategy, or service and the intended outcomes?

660. What would the impact to the Privacy Engineering project objectives be should the risk arise?

661. How often will the Risk Management Plan and Risk Register be formally reviewed, and by whom?

662. What action, if any, has been taken to respond to the risk?

663. What risks might negatively or positively affect achieving the Privacy Engineering project objectives?

664. How well are risks controlled?

665. What is the probability and impact of the risk occurring?

666. How could corresponding Risk affect the Privacy Engineering project in terms of cost and schedule?

667. Have other controls and solutions been implemented in other services which could be applied as an alternative to additional funding?

668. Are your objectives at risk?

669. What should you do now?

670. What are the assumptions and current status that support the assessment of the risk?

671. Why would you develop a risk register?

672. What should the audit role be in establishing a risk management process?

673. What will be done?

674. What are the major risks facing the Privacy Engineering project?

2.33 Probability and Impact Assessment: Privacy Engineering

675. Is the customer technically sophisticated in the product area?

676. Is the technology to be built new to your organization?

677. What is the likelihood?

678. How do the products attain the specifications?

679. How are the local factors going to affect the absorption?

680. What action do you usually take against risks?

681. What risks does the employee encounter?

682. How will the consumption pattern change?

683. Are the risk data timely and relevant?

684. Do you have a mechanism for managing change?

685. Who should be notified of the occurrence of each of the risk indicators?

686. To what extent is the chosen technology maturing?

687. Prioritized components/features?

688. Does the software interface with new or unproven hardware or unproven vendor products?

689. What should be the level of coordination?

690. What significant shift will occur in governmental policies, laws, and regulations pertaining to specific industries?

691. What is the likely future demand of the customer?

692. Does the customer have a solid idea of what is required?

693. How would you assess the risk management process in the Privacy Engineering project?

694. Is security a central objective?

2.34 Probability and Impact Matrix: Privacy Engineering

695. What can you do about it?

696. Will there be an increase in the political conservatism?

697. How carefully have the potential competitors been identified?

698. Are compilers and code generators available and suitable for the product to be built?

699. What is the impact if the risk does occur?

700. What new technologies are being explored in the same area?

701. What is the probability of the risk occurring?

702. Do you need a risk management plan?

703. Can you avoid altogether some things that might go wrong?

704. How is the risk management process used in practice?

705. Are you on schedule?

706. Several experts are offsite, and wish to be included. How can this be done?

707. Brain storm – mind maps, what if?

708. Amount of reused software?

709. Are staff committed for the duration of the Privacy Engineering project?

710. What are the levels of understanding of the future users of this technology?

2.35 Risk Data Sheet: Privacy Engineering

711. Do effective diagnostic tests exist?

712. Potential for recurrence?

713. What are you trying to achieve (Objectives)?

714. What are the main opportunities available to you that you should grab while you can?

715. What is the environment within which you operate (social trends, economic, community values, broad based participation, national directions etc.)?

716. Whom do you serve (customers)?

717. What were the Causes that contributed?

718. What can happen?

719. How do you handle product safely?

720. Type of risk identified?

721. What can you do?

722. Has the most cost-effective solution been chosen?

723. How reliable is the data source?

724. Is the data sufficiently specified in terms of the type of failure being analyzed, and its frequency or probability?

725. What are you here for (Mission)?

726. Has a sensitivity analysis been carried out?

727. What do people affected think about the need for, and practicality of preventive measures?

728. What are the main threats to your existence?

2.36 Procurement Management Plan: Privacy Engineering

729. Are parking lot items captured?

730. Has a Privacy Engineering project Communications Plan been developed?

731. Are any non-compliance issues that exist communicated to your organization?

732. Are the quality tools and methods identified in the Quality Plan appropriate to the Privacy Engineering project?

733. Is the Privacy Engineering project schedule available for all Privacy Engineering project team members to review?

734. Have the key elements of a coherent Privacy Engineering project management strategy been established?

735. Was your organizations estimating methodology being used and followed?

736. Are change requests logged and managed?

737. Do Privacy Engineering project managers participating in the Privacy Engineering project know the Privacy Engineering projects true status first hand?

738. Are trade-offs between accepting the risk and mitigating the risk identified?

739. Does the Privacy Engineering project team have the right skills?

740. Sensitivity analysis?

741. Have activity relationships and interdependencies within tasks been adequately identified?

742. Is there a Steering Committee in place?

743. Are adequate resources provided for the quality assurance function?

744. Public engagement – did you get it right?

745. Are all resource assumptions documented?

2.37 Source Selection Criteria: Privacy Engineering

746. When is it appropriate to issue a DRFP?

747. What should be considered?

748. With the rapid changes in information technology, will media be readable in five or ten years?

749. What are the limitations on pre-competitive range communications?

750. What aspects should the contracting officer brief the Privacy Engineering project on prior to evaluation of proposals?

751. How much weight should be placed on past performance information?

752. When must you conduct a debriefing?

753. Are there any specific considerations that precludes offers from being selected as the awardee?

754. Are there any common areas of weaknesses or deficiencies in the proposals in the competitive range?

755. Which contract type places the most risk on the seller?

756. What should a Draft Request for Proposal (DRFP) include?

757. Is the offeror pricing what is technically proposed?

758. When is it appropriate to issue a Draft Request for Proposal (DRFP)?

759. How long will it take for the purchase cost to be the same as the lease cost?

760. What information may not be provided?

761. Why promote competition?

762. Is there collaboration among your evaluators?

763. What is cost analysis and when should it be performed?

764. What documentation is needed for a tradeoff decision?

765. Have team members been adequately trained?

2.38 Stakeholder Management Plan: Privacy Engineering

766. Is quality monitored from the perspective of the customers needs and expectations?

767. What is to be the method of release?

768. Do Privacy Engineering project teams & team members report on status / activities / progress?

769. Has a provision been made to reassess Privacy Engineering project risks at various Privacy Engineering project stages?

770. Are changes in deliverable commitments agreed to by all affected groups & individuals?

771. Have the key elements of a coherent Privacy Engineering project management strategy been established?

772. What potential impact does the stakeholder have on the Privacy Engineering project?

773. Is an industry recognized mechanized support tool(s) being used for Privacy Engineering project scheduling & tracking?

774. Has the Privacy Engineering project scope been baselined?

775. Who will be responsible for managing and

maintaining the Issues Register?

776. Are updated Privacy Engineering project time & resource estimates reasonable based on the current Privacy Engineering project stage?

777. Have Privacy Engineering project success criteria been defined?

778. What preventative action can be taken to reduce the likelihood a risk will be realised?

779. Was trending evident between reviews?

780. Does a documented Privacy Engineering project organizational policy & plan (i.e. governance model) exist?

2.39 Change Management Plan: Privacy Engineering

781. What new behaviours are required?

782. What tasks are needed?

783. What risks may occur upfront?

784. How much Privacy Engineering project management is needed?

785. Identify the current level of skills and knowledge and behaviours of the group that will be impacted on. What prerequisite knowledge do corresponding groups need?

786. Has the training co-ordinator been provided with the training details and put in place the necessary arrangements?

787. What communication network would you use – informal or formal?

788. What is the reason for the communication?

789. Do there need to be new channels developed?

790. What are the responsibilities assigned to each role?

791. Have the business unit contacts been selected and notified?

792. How badly can information be misinterpreted?

793. How frequently should you repeat the message?

794. Is there an adequate supply of people for the new roles?

795. How far reaching in your organization is the change?

796. When to start change management?

797. Has a training need analysis been carried out?

798. Who in the business it includes?

799. Has the priority for this Privacy Engineering project been set by the Business Unit Management Team?

3.0 Executing Process Group: Privacy Engineering

800. Are the necessary foundations in place to ensure the sustainability of the results of the programme?

801. After how many days will the lease cost be the same as the purchase cost for the equipment?

802. Are escalated issues resolved promptly?

803. In what way has the program come up with innovative measures for problem-solving?

804. Is the schedule for the set products being met?

805. Would you rate yourself as being risk-averse, risk-neutral, or risk-seeking?

806. Based on your Privacy Engineering project communication management plan, what worked well?

807. What are the key components of the Privacy Engineering project communications plan?

808. Do your results resemble a normal distribution?

809. How do you measure difficulty?

810. Who are the Privacy Engineering project stakeholders?

811. How well did the team follow the chosen processes?

812. What type of people would you want on your team?

813. How can you use Microsoft Privacy Engineering project and Excel to assist in Privacy Engineering project risk management?

814. Have operating capacities been created and/or reinforced in partners?

815. What are the Privacy Engineering project management deliverables of each process group?

816. What areas were overlooked on this Privacy Engineering project?

817. What will you do to minimize the impact should a risk event occur?

818. Will additional funds be needed for hardware or software?

3.1 Team Member Status Report: Privacy Engineering

819. Are your organizations Privacy Engineering projects more successful over time?

820. How much risk is involved?

821. Does your organization have the means (staff, money, contract, etc.) to produce or to acquire the product, good, or service?

822. What specific interest groups do you have in place?

823. Will the staff do training or is that done by a third party?

824. When a teams productivity and success depend on collaboration and the efficient flow of information, what generally fails them?

825. Does the product, good, or service already exist within your organization?

826. The problem with Reward & Recognition Programs is that the truly deserving people all too often get left out. How can you make it practical?

827. Do you have an Enterprise Privacy Engineering project Management Office (EPMO)?

828. Does every department have to have a Privacy

Engineering project Manager on staff?

829. Why is it to be done?

830. How will resource planning be done?

831. What is to be done?

832. How it is to be done?

833. Are the attitudes of staff regarding Privacy Engineering project work improving?

834. How does this product, good, or service meet the needs of the Privacy Engineering project and your organization as a whole?

835. How can you make it practical?

836. Are the products of your organizations Privacy Engineering projects meeting customers objectives?

837. Is there evidence that staff is taking a more professional approach toward management of your organizations Privacy Engineering projects?

3.2 Change Request: Privacy Engineering

838. Who is communicating the change?

839. How can you ensure that changes have been made properly?

840. How is quality being addressed on the Privacy Engineering project?

841. How are changes requested (forms, method of communication)?

842. Is it feasible to use requirements attributes as predictors of reliability?

843. Where do changes come from?

844. Which requirements attributes affect the risk to reliability the most?

845. Will all change requests and current status be logged?

846. What are the requirements for urgent changes?

847. How do you get changes (code) out in a timely manner?

848. Who can suggest changes?

849. Who is included in the change control team?

850. Has your address changed?

851. What mechanism is used to appraise others of changes that are made?

852. Who needs to approve change requests?

853. How is the change documented (format, content, storage)?

854. What is the function of the change control committee?

855. Are there requirements attributes that are strongly related to the occurrence of defects and failures?

3.3 Change Log: Privacy Engineering

856. Is the change request open, closed or pending?

857. Is the change backward compatible without limitations?

858. How does this relate to the standards developed for specific business processes?

859. Is this a mandatory replacement?

860. How does this change affect the timeline of the schedule?

861. Is the requested change request a result of changes in other Privacy Engineering project(s)?

862. Who initiated the change request?

863. Does the suggested change request represent a desired enhancement to the products functionality?

864. Will the Privacy Engineering project fail if the change request is not executed?

865. Is the change request within Privacy Engineering project scope?

866. Does the suggested change request seem to represent a necessary enhancement to the product?

867. Do the described changes impact on the integrity or security of the system?

868. When was the request approved?

869. Is the submitted change a new change or a modification of a previously approved change?

870. How does this change affect scope?

871. When was the request submitted?

3.4 Decision Log: Privacy Engineering

872. Meeting purpose; why does this team meet?

873. How effective is maintaining the log at facilitating organizational learning?

874. Linked to original objective?

875. How does an increasing emphasis on cost containment influence the strategies and tactics used?

876. What eDiscovery problem or issue did your organization set out to fix or make better?

877. Do strategies and tactics aimed at less than full control reduce the costs of management or simply shift the cost burden?

878. Behaviors; what are guidelines that the team has identified that will assist them with getting the most out of team meetings?

879. How do you define success?

880. What are the cost implications?

881. What is the average size of your matters in an applicable measurement?

882. What was the rationale for the decision?

883. What makes you different or better than others

companies selling the same thing?

884. Decision-making process; how will the team make decisions?

885. Who will be given a copy of this document and where will it be kept?

886. Adversarial environment. is your opponent open to a non-traditional workflow, or will it likely challenge anything you do?

887. It becomes critical to track and periodically revisit both operational effectiveness; Are you noticing all that you need to, and are you interpreting what you see effectively?

888. How does provision of information, both in terms of content and presentation, influence acceptance of alternative strategies?

889. How do you know when you are achieving it?

890. What is the line where eDiscovery ends and document review begins?

891. Which variables make a critical difference?

3.5 Quality Audit: Privacy Engineering

892. Do prior clients have a positive opinion of your organization?

893. How does your organization know that its staff entrance standards are appropriately effective and constructive and being implemented consistently?

894. How does your organization know that its Strategic Plan is providing the best guidance for the future of your organization?

895. How does the organization know that its industry and community engagement planning and management systems are appropriately effective and constructive in enabling relationships with key stakeholder groups?

896. How does your organization know that its support services planning and management systems are appropriately effective and constructive?

897. How does your organization know that its system for recruiting the best staff possible are appropriately effective and constructive?

898. How does your organization know that its teaching activities (and staff learning) are effectively and constructively enhanced by its activities?

899. How does your organization know whether they are adhering to mission and achieving objectives?

900. How does your organization know that its staff are presenting original work, and properly acknowledging the work of others?

901. How does your organization know that its public relations and marketing systems are appropriately effective and constructive?

902. What are the main things that hinder your ability to do a good job?

903. What does an analysis of your organizations staff profile suggest in terms of its planning, and how is this being addressed?

904. Is progress against the intentions measurable?

905. Are the policies and processes, as set out in the Quality Audit Manual, properly applied?

906. Are all employees made aware of device defects which may occur from the improper performance of specific jobs?

907. How does your organization know that it provides a safe and healthy environment?

908. How does your organization know that its research programs are appropriately effective and constructive?

909. How does your organization know that the review processes are effective?

910. Have personnel cleanliness and health requirements been established?

911. Is there any content that may be legally actionable?

3.6 Team Directory: Privacy Engineering

912. Days from the time the issue is identified?

913. Process decisions: do job conditions warrant additional actions to collect job information and document on-site activity?

914. Timing: when do the effects of communication take place?

915. What are you going to deliver or accomplish?

916. Process decisions: how well was task order work performed?

917. Who will report Privacy Engineering project status to all stakeholders?

918. Who should receive information (all stakeholders)?

919. Who will write the meeting minutes and distribute?

920. Contract requirements complied with?

921. Have you decided when to celebrate the Privacy Engineering projects completion date?

922. Who will talk to the customer?

923. Who are the Team Members?

924. Process decisions: are there any statutory or regulatory issues relevant to the timely execution of work?

925. Process decisions: are all start-up, turn over and close out requirements of the contract satisfied?

926. Decisions: is the most suitable form of contract being used?

927. Decisions: what could be done better to improve the quality of the constructed product?

928. When will you produce deliverables?

929. How will the team handle changes?

3.7 Team Operating Agreement: Privacy Engineering

930. Are there the right people on your team?

931. What is group supervision?

932. The method to be used in the decision making process; Will it be consensus, majority rule, or the supervisor having the final say?

933. Do you solicit member feedback about meetings and what would make them better?

934. How will your group handle planned absences?

935. Do you begin with a question to engage everyone?

936. What went well?

937. What are the boundaries (organizational or geographic) within which you operate?

938. Do you post any action items, due dates, and responsibilities on the team website?

939. What are the current caseload numbers in the unit?

940. To whom do you deliver your services?

941. How will you divide work equitably?

942. What types of accommodations will be formulated and put in place for sustaining the team?

943. Do you upload presentation materials in advance and test the technology?

944. What is a Virtual Team?

945. Do team members reside in more than two countries?

946. How will group handle unplanned absences?

947. Do you vary your voice pace, tone and pitch to engage participants and gain involvement?

948. Are there more than two national cultures represented by your team?

949. Are there more than two functional areas represented by your team?

3.8 Team Performance Assessment: Privacy Engineering

950. To what degree will the team ensure that all members equitably share the work essential to the success of the team?

951. To what degree will the team adopt a concrete, clearly understood, and agreed-upon approach that will result in achievement of the teams goals?

952. To what degree will the approach capitalize on and enhance the skills of all team members in a manner that takes into consideration other demands on members of the team?

953. To what degree can the team measure progress against specific goals?

954. If you are worried about method variance before you collect data, what sort of design elements might you include to reduce or eliminate the threat of method variance?

955. How hard did you try to make a good selection?

956. What makes opportunities more or less obvious?

957. Lack of method variance in self-reported affect and perceptions at work: Reality or artifact?

958. To what degree will team members, individually and collectively, commit time to help themselves and

others learn and develop skills?

959. To what degree do all members feel responsible for all agreed-upon measures?

960. Is there a particular method of data analysis that you would recommend as a means of demonstrating that method variance is not of great concern for a given dataset?

961. Which situations call for a more extreme type of adaptiveness in which team members actually re-define roles?

962. To what degree does the teams purpose constitute a broader, deeper aspiration than just accomplishing short-term goals?

963. How do you manage human resources?

964. What structural changes have you made or are you preparing to make?

965. To what degree will new and supplemental skills be introduced as the need is recognized?

966. To what degree are the goals ambitious?

967. To what degree do team members frequently explore the teams purpose and its implications?

968. To what degree can team members frequently and easily communicate with one another?

969. To what degree are fresh input and perspectives systematically caught and added (for example,

through information and analysis, new members, and
senior sponsors)?

3.9 Team Member Performance Assessment: Privacy Engineering

970. What is a general description of the processes under performance measurement and assessment?

971. How is the timing of assessments organized (e.g., pre/post-test, single point during training, multiple reassessment during training)?

972. Who they are?

973. What kinds of performance factors / elements do you use?

974. Who should attend?

975. Can your organization rate by exception and assume that most employees are performing at an acceptable level?

976. How do you use data to inform instruction and improve staff achievement?

977. Has the appropriate access to relevant data and analysis capability been granted?

978. How is performance assessment used in making future award decisions including options and extend/compete decisions?

979. Do the goals support your organizations goals?

980. How often are assessments to be conducted?

981. To what degree is the team cognizant of small wins to be celebrated along the way?

982. To what extent are systems and applications (e.g., game engine, mobile device platform) utilized?

983. To what degree do team members articulate the teams work approach?

984. Why do performance reviews?

985. What is the large, desired outcome?

986. Verify business objectives. Are they appropriate, and well-articulated?

987. To what degree are the skill areas critical to team performance present?

988. Should a ratee get a copy of all the raters documents about the employees performance?

3.10 Issue Log: Privacy Engineering

989. How much time does it take to do it?

990. Why do you manage human resources?

991. What steps can you take for positive relationships?

992. How do you manage communications?

993. Are you constantly rushing from meeting to meeting?

994. Who are the members of the governing body?

995. Who is involved as you identify stakeholders?

996. Who reported the issue?

997. Why multiple evaluators?

998. What approaches do you use?

999. Do you feel a register helps?

1000. Are they needed?

1001. How do you reply to this question; you am new here and managing this major program. How do you suggest you build your network?

1002. What date was the issue resolved?

1003. Persistence; will users learn a work around or will they be bothered every time?

1004. Who were proponents/opponents?

4.0 Monitoring and Controlling Process Group: Privacy Engineering

1005. How is agile program management done?

1006. Who needs to be engaged upfront to ensure use of results?

1007. How many more potential communications channels were introduced by the discovery of the new stakeholders?

1008. Based on your Privacy Engineering project communication management plan, what worked well?

1009. Is it what was agreed upon?

1010. How well did the chosen processes produce the expected results?

1011. How will staff learn how to use the deliverables?

1012. Did you implement the program as designed?

1013. Were escalated issues resolved promptly?

1014. What business situation is being addressed?

1015. What areas were overlooked on this Privacy Engineering project?

1016. What is the timeline?

1017. How well defined and documented were the Privacy Engineering project management processes you chose to use?

1018. How was the program set-up initiated?

1019. How should needs be met?

4.1 Project Performance Report: Privacy Engineering

1020. To what degree do the goals specify concrete team work products?

1021. To what degree does the formal organization make use of individual resources and meet individual needs?

1022. To what degree do individual skills and abilities match task demands?

1023. To what degree do the structures of the formal organization motivate taskrelevant behavior and facilitate task completion?

1024. To what degree does the teams approach to its work allow for modification and improvement over time?

1025. To what degree can the cognitive capacity of individuals accommodate the flow of information?

1026. How is the data used?

1027. To what degree are the structures of the formal organization consistent with the behaviors in the informal organization?

1028. What is the PRS?

1029. To what degree does the information network

communicate information relevant to the task?

1030. What is the degree to which rules govern information exchange between groups?

1031. To what degree does the teams work approach provide opportunity for members to engage in results-based evaluation?

1032. To what degree is there centralized control of information sharing?

1033. To what degree are the members clear on what they are individually responsible for and what they are jointly responsible for?

1034. To what degree can the team ensure that all members are individually and jointly accountable for the teams purpose, goals, approach, and work-products?

1035. How will procurement be coordinated with other Privacy Engineering project aspects, such as scheduling and performance reporting?

4.2 Variance Analysis: Privacy Engineering

1036. Are there knowledgeable Privacy Engineering projections of future performance?

1037. Do you identify potential or actual budget-based and time-based schedule variances?

1038. How are material, labor, and overhead variances calculated and recorded?

1039. Does the scheduling system identify in a timely manner the status of work?

1040. How do you identify potential or actual overruns and underruns?

1041. Are indirect costs accumulated for comparison with the corresponding budgets?

1042. Why do variances exist?

1043. Did a new competitor enter the market?

1044. What causes selling price variance?

1045. How does your organization allocate the cost of shared expenses and services?

1046. How do you verify authorization to proceed with all authorized work?

1047. There are detailed schedules which support control account and work package start and completion dates/events?

1048. Are all cwbs elements specified for external reporting?

1049. What is the expected future profitability of each customer?

1050. Are material costs reported within the same period as that in which BCWP is earned for that material?

1051. Contract line items and end items?

1052. When, during the last four quarters, did a primary business event occur causing a fluctuation?

4.3 Earned Value Status: Privacy Engineering

1053. Validation is a process of ensuring that the developed system will actually achieve the stakeholders desired outcomes; Are you building the right product? What do you validate?

1054. Earned value can be used in almost any Privacy Engineering project situation and in almost any Privacy Engineering project environment. it may be used on large Privacy Engineering projects, medium sized Privacy Engineering projects, tiny Privacy Engineering projects (in cut-down form), complex and simple Privacy Engineering projects and in any market sector. some people, of course, know all about earned value, they have used it for years - but perhaps not as effectively as they could have?

1055. How does this compare with other Privacy Engineering projects?

1056. Where is evidence-based earned value in your organization reported?

1057. Where are your problem areas?

1058. What is the unit of forecast value?

1059. If earned value management (EVM) is so good in determining the true status of a Privacy Engineering project and Privacy Engineering project its completion, why is it that hardly any one uses it in information systems related Privacy Engineering projects?

1060. How much is it going to cost by the finish?

1061. Are you hitting your Privacy Engineering projects targets?

1062. When is it going to finish?

1063. Verification is a process of ensuring that the developed system satisfies the stakeholders agreements and specifications; Are you building the product right? What do you verify?

4.4 Risk Audit: Privacy Engineering

1064. Should additional substantive testing be conducted because of the risk audit results?

1065. How do you manage risk?

1066. Have all involved been advised of any obligations they have to sponsors?

1067. Are there any forms the staff is required to sign?

1068. Are all managers or operators of the facility or equipment competent or qualified?

1069. Do your financial policies and procedures ensure that each step in financial handling (receipt, recording, banking, reporting) is not completed by one person?

1070. Are team members trained in the use of the tools?

1071. Have staff received necessary training?

1072. What does internal control mean in the context of the audit process?

1073. To what extent should analytical procedures be utilized in the risk-assessment process?

1074. Are enough people available?

1075. Management -what contingency plans do you

have if the risk becomes a reality?

1076. Are procedures developed to respond to foreseeable emergencies and communicated to all involved?

1077. Are Privacy Engineering project requirements stable?

1078. To what extent are auditors effective at linking business risks and management assertions?

1079. Do you manage the process through use of metrics?

1080. Will an appropriate standard of care be applied to all involved?

1081. How can the strategy fail/achieved?

4.5 Contractor Status Report: Privacy Engineering

1082. What was the overall budget or estimated cost?

1083. Describe how often regular updates are made to the proposed solution. Are corresponding regular updates included in the standard maintenance plan?

1084. Who can list a Privacy Engineering project as organization experience, your organization or a previous employee of your organization?

1085. What process manages the contracts?

1086. Are there contractual transfer concerns?

1087. How does the proposed individual meet each requirement?

1088. What was the final actual cost?

1089. How long have you been using the services?

1090. What are the minimum and optimal bandwidth requirements for the proposed solution?

1091. What was the actual budget or estimated cost for your organizations services?

1092. How is risk transferred?

1093. If applicable; describe your standard schedule

for new software version releases. Are new software version releases included in the standard maintenance plan?

1094. What is the average response time for answering a support call?

1095. What was the budget or estimated cost for your organizations services?

4.6 Formal Acceptance: Privacy Engineering

1096. What are the requirements against which to test, Who will execute?

1097. Do you buy-in installation services?

1098. Have all comments been addressed?

1099. What function(s) does it fill or meet?

1100. Do you perform formal acceptance or burn-in tests?

1101. Was business value realized?

1102. How does your team plan to obtain formal acceptance on your Privacy Engineering project?

1103. Was the Privacy Engineering project managed well?

1104. Do you buy pre-configured systems or build your own configuration?

1105. Who supplies data?

1106. What can you do better next time?

1107. What features, practices, and processes proved to be strengths or weaknesses?

1108. Was the client satisfied with the Privacy Engineering project results?

1109. Does it do what client said it would?

1110. Did the Privacy Engineering project achieve its MOV?

1111. What is the Acceptance Management Process?

1112. Was the sponsor/customer satisfied?

1113. Does it do what Privacy Engineering project team said it would?

1114. Was the Privacy Engineering project work done on time, within budget, and according to specification?

1115. Was the Privacy Engineering project goal achieved?

5.0 Closing Process Group: Privacy Engineering

1116. Is the Privacy Engineering project funded?

1117. What was learned?

1118. What is an Encumbrance?

1119. Did you do what you said you were going to do?

1120. Who are the Privacy Engineering project stakeholders?

1121. What were the desired outcomes?

1122. Will the Privacy Engineering project deliverable(s) replace a current asset or group of assets?

1123. Is the Privacy Engineering project funded?

1124. What is the Privacy Engineering project name and date of completion?

1125. How dependent is the Privacy Engineering project on other Privacy Engineering projects or work efforts?

1126. Is this a follow-on to a previous Privacy Engineering project?

1127. How will you do it?

5.1 Procurement Audit: Privacy Engineering

1128. Does the contract meet criteria of completeness and consistency?

1129. Are there systems for recording and managing stocks (where part of contract)?

1130. Are fixed asset accounts posted currently?

1131. Is each copy of the purchase order necessary?

1132. Are there appropriate controls in place to ensure that procurement complies with the relevant legislation?

1133. Has your organization fulfilled its obligations related to the payment of social security contributions and taxes?

1134. Does the strategy include a policy for identifying and training suitable procurement staff?

1135. Are sub-criteria clearly indicated?

1136. Is there no evidence of collusion between bidders?

1137. Was a formal review of tenders received undertaken?

1138. In case of decisions not to conclude a

procurement or award a contract, were tenderers informed in writing and on a timely basis of the already stated decisions and grounds?

1139. Are staff members evaluated in accordance with the terms of existing negotiated agreements?

1140. Does the procurement function/unit understand costumer needs, supply markets and suppliers?

1141. Have guidelines been set up for how the procurement process should be conducted?

1142. Are there special emergency purchase order procedures?

1143. Are checks used in numeric sequence?

1144. Are the financial and business records of your organization stored in a secure fire resistant place?

1145. Are employees with cash disbursement responsibilities required to take scheduled vacations?

1146. Is the weighting set coherent, convincing and leaving little scope for arbitrary and random evaluation and ranking?

1147. If a purchase order calls for a cost-plus agreement, is the method of determining how final charges will be determined specified?

5.2 Contract Close-Out: Privacy Engineering

1148. Change in knowledge?

1149. Change in circumstances?

1150. Have all contract records been included in the Privacy Engineering project archives?

1151. Have all contracts been closed?

1152. Was the contract type appropriate?

1153. Parties: who is involved?

1154. Parties: Authorized?

1155. Change in attitude or behavior?

1156. What happens to the recipient of services?

1157. How/when used ?

1158. Have all acceptance criteria been met prior to final payment to contractors?

1159. Was the contract sufficiently clear so as not to result in numerous disputes and misunderstandings?

1160. How does it work?

1161. Has each contract been audited to verify

acceptance and delivery?

1162. Why Outsource?

1163. Have all contracts been completed?

1164. Are the signers the authorized officials?

1165. How is the contracting office notified of the automatic contract close-out?

1166. What is capture management?

1167. Was the contract complete without requiring numerous changes and revisions?

5.3 Project or Phase Close-Out: Privacy Engineering

1168. Did the delivered product meet the specified requirements and goals of the Privacy Engineering project?

1169. Who are the Privacy Engineering project stakeholders and what are roles and involvement?

1170. Have business partners been involved extensively, and what data was required for them?

1171. What are the informational communication needs for each stakeholder?

1172. In addition to assessing whether the Privacy Engineering project was successful, it is equally critical to analyze why it was or was not fully successful. Are you including this?

1173. In preparing the Lessons Learned report, should it reflect a consensus viewpoint, or should the report reflect the different individual viewpoints?

1174. What could have been improved?

1175. What is a Risk?

1176. When and how were information needs best met?

1177. What is a Risk Management Process?

1178. Planned remaining costs?

1179. Does the lesson educate others to improve performance?

1180. If you were the Privacy Engineering project sponsor, how would you determine which Privacy Engineering project team(s) and/or individuals deserve recognition?

1181. Which changes might a stakeholder be required to make as a result of the Privacy Engineering project?

1182. What security considerations needed to be addressed during the procurement life cycle?

1183. Was the user/client satisfied with the end product?

1184. What hierarchical authority does the stakeholder have in your organization?

1185. Is there a clear cause and effect between the activity and the lesson learned?

5.4 Lessons Learned: Privacy Engineering

1186. Is there any way in which you think your development process hampered this Privacy Engineering project?

1187. Did the Privacy Engineering project management methodology work?

1188. Why does your organization need a lessons learned (LL) capability?

1189. How does the budget cycle affect the case?

1190. How comprehensive was integration testing?

1191. What were the major enablers to a quick response?

1192. What would you approach differently next time?

1193. Was Privacy Engineering project performance validated or challenged?

1194. Do you have any real problems?

1195. For the next Privacy Engineering project, how could you improve on the way Privacy Engineering project was conducted?

1196. How effective were your design reviews?

1197. What if anything has been lacking?

1198. How well did the scope of the Privacy Engineering project match what was defined in the Privacy Engineering project Proposal?

1199. How satisfied are you with your involvement in the development and/or review of the Privacy Engineering project Scope during Privacy Engineering project Initiation and Planning?

1200. Where could you improve?

1201. How much of your time was spent on other than this Privacy Engineering project?

1202. What were the main sources of frustration in the Privacy Engineering project?

1203. Overall, how effective was the performance of the Privacy Engineering project Manager?

1204. What would you like to see better documented about how to use existing processes on this type of Privacy Engineering project?

1205. What is the quality and content of communication?

Index

crucial 66
crystal 10
culture 33, 65, 181, 187-188
cultures   227
current 27, 43, 46, 53, 60, 67, 71, 78, 86, 94, 107, 109, 120, 145,
183, 185, 196, 208-209, 215, 226, 249
currently   41, 119, 250
custom 22
customer   18, 28, 32-33, 35, 39, 82, 92, 100, 112-113, 116,
127, 140, 144, 177, 180, 193-194, 197-198, 224, 240, 248
customers   1, 24, 29-30, 45-46, 52, 57, 67, 71, 94, 104, 108,
110-111, 115, 118, 121, 143, 145, 201, 207, 214
cut-down   241
cycles 126
damage   1
Dashboard   8
dashboards   97
dataset   229
day-to-day   95, 109
deadlines   23, 112, 158
dealing   22
debriefing   205
decide 187
decided   108, 224
deciding   118
decision   5, 53, 81-82, 85, 87, 189, 206, 219, 226
decisions   77-79, 83, 85-86, 92, 99, 101, 124, 187, 220, 224-
225, 231, 250-251
decomposed 165
dedicated   7
deeper   10, 229
defects   179, 216, 222
define 2, 26, 33, 35, 41, 59, 72, 87, 148, 188, 219
defined   10, 15, 19-20, 26, 29-34, 36-37, 43, 58, 60, 64, 75,
91, 103, 124, 132, 144-145, 147, 150, 153, 169, 172, 181, 186-187,
190, 208, 236, 257
defines 21, 28, 36
defining   7, 121, 136
definite   100
definition   16, 26, 35-36, 40-41, 177
degree   228-229, 232, 237-238
delayed   158
delaying   51

enhancing 94
enough 7, 61, 112, 140-141, 243
ensure 35, 38, 59, 66, 108, 110, 117, 126, 131, 152, 165, 183-184, 211, 215, 228, 235, 238, 243, 250
ensures 117
ensuring 9, 119, 131, 241-242
entail 51
Enterprise 213
entire 150
entities 54
entity 1
entrance 221
equally 254
equipment 17, 24, 179, 211, 243
equipped 29
equitably 28, 226, 228
errors 119, 150, 179
escalated 211, 235
essential 75, 228
establish 75, 93, 175, 180
estimate 46, 52-53, 133-134, 167, 169, 171
estimated 38, 40, 49, 53, 113, 175, 245-246
estimates 3-4, 36, 47, 61, 133-134, 149-150, 165, 169, 171-173, 177, 208
Estimating 4, 167, 175-176, 203
estimation 86, 135, 153, 172
estimator 173
etcetera 52, 109
ethical 121
ethnic 115
evaluate 76, 144, 149
evaluated 165, 178, 251
evaluating 77, 166
evaluation 60, 83, 87, 95, 133, 181, 205, 238, 251
evaluators 206, 233
events 16, 81, 89, 149, 240
everyday 73
everyone 28, 39, 181, 183, 226
everything 43
evidence 10, 52, 195, 214, 250
evident 208
evolution 43
evolve 101

locally 79
logged203, 215
logical 161-162
longer 93
long-term   101, 107, 110
Looking   17
losing   52
losses   16
lowest 160
magnitude   82
maintain   91, 114, 180
maintained   81, 150
majority   226
makers85, 97, 189
making   25, 78, 81, 119, 226, 231
manage   29, 39, 41, 44-45, 50, 59, 66, 76-77, 81-82, 87, 106,
126, 137, 141, 156, 178, 180, 229, 233, 243-244
manageable 26, 84, 165
managed   7, 32, 58, 62, 76, 82, 89, 91, 97, 144, 153, 203, 247
management 1, 3-5, 8-9, 17-19, 31, 38-39, 57, 60-61, 63, 69, 72,
78-80, 83, 87-88, 106, 113, 116, 124, 131-137, 143-145, 149-150,
152, 163, 165-166, 170-171, 173, 177-179, 183, 186, 189, 191-193,
195-196, 198-199, 203, 207, 209-214, 219, 221, 235-236, 241, 243-
244, 248, 253-254, 256
manager   7, 9, 21, 38, 40, 116, 137, 172, 214, 257
managers   2, 123, 134, 150, 189, 193, 203, 243
manages   79, 82, 245
managing   2, 80, 123, 128, 166, 169, 197, 207, 233, 250
mandatory   217
manner   16, 79, 124, 146, 149, 151, 215, 228, 239
mantle 112
Manual   179, 222
mapped   34
Mapping   58, 64
market 18, 158, 194-195, 239, 241
marketable   194-195
marketer   7
marketing   104, 145, 159, 222
markets   17, 251
material   150, 181, 239-240
materials   1, 227
matrices   141
Matrix 2-4, 129, 141, 185, 199

product   1, 53, 67, 71, 107, 109, 137, 158, 177-178, 194-195, 197, 199, 201, 213-214, 217, 225, 241-242, 254-255
production   38, 83, 105, 145
productive   185
products   1, 24, 56, 115, 117, 126, 129, 131, 141, 173, 197-198, 211, 214, 217, 237
profile 222
program   17, 53, 72, 97, 131-132, 134, 173, 179, 211, 233, 235-236
programme   211
programs   213, 222
progress   35, 49, 91, 119, 124, 171, 175, 189, 207, 222, 228
prohibited   150
project 2-8, 18-19, 22, 34, 55, 59, 61, 68, 88, 91, 94, 99-100, 107, 109, 112-114, 116-118, 121, 123-139, 141, 143-144, 147-149, 152-158, 160-161, 163, 165-173, 175-178, 185, 188-190, 192-196, 198, 200, 203-205, 207-215, 217, 224, 235-238, 241, 244-245, 247-249, 252, 254-257
projected   185
projects   2, 57, 106, 109, 123, 127, 131, 141, 144, 148, 166, 169, 171, 180, 187, 189, 203, 213-214, 224, 241-242, 249
promising   109
promote   56, 58, 206
promptly   211, 235
proofing   79
proper 94, 137, 186
properly   34, 39, 124, 140, 150, 215, 222
proponents   234
Proposal   206, 257
proposals   97, 166, 205
proposed   19, 49, 52, 133, 139, 206, 245
protect   69, 118
protected   63
protection   116
protocols   182
proved 247
provide   17, 70, 109-110, 119, 128, 149, 168, 170, 176, 185-186, 238
provided   11, 98, 152, 171, 204, 206, 209
providers   84
provides   139, 158, 164, 222
providing   94, 128, 143, 177, 221
provision   153, 189, 207, 220

public 204, 222
publisher 1
pulled 106
purchase 7, 206, 211, 250-251
purchased 150
purpose 2, 9, 120, 126, 164, 170, 176, 183, 219, 229, 238
purposes 127
qualified 28, 59, 67, 71, 243
qualifies 68, 71
qualify 55, 69
qualities 17
quality 1, 4-5, 9, 21, 44, 47, 50, 61-62, 68, 70, 88, 92, 102, 108,
136, 152-153, 165, 169-171, 179-184, 187-188, 203-204, 207, 215,
221-222, 225, 257
quantify 55
quarters 240
question 10, 15, 26, 43, 58, 75, 91, 103, 117, 226, 233
questions 7-8, 10, 71, 138, 167
quickly 9, 60, 66, 73
random 251
ranking251
raters 232
rather 104
rational 151
rationale 219
reached 17, 135
reaching 210
reactivate 107
readable 205
readiness 38
readings 99, 131
realised 208
realistic 17, 59, 115, 133
reality 178, 228, 244
realize 56
realized 247
really 7, 20, 27
real-world 70
reason 120, 209
reasonable 84, 133, 208
reasons 35
reassess 153, 189, 207
re-assign 156

specific   8, 20, 30, 34, 39, 65, 114, 135, 144, 155-157, 162-163, 187, 198, 205, 213, 217, 222, 228
specified   152, 202, 240, 251, 254
specify 237
spoken 112
sponsor   18, 133, 144, 248, 255
sponsored   37
sponsors   24, 189, 230, 243
spread 99, 102
stable 193, 244
staffed 40
staffing 20, 97, 134
stages 153, 189, 207
standard   7, 92, 101, 162, 166, 182, 244-246
standards   1, 9-10, 93, 95-96, 98, 135, 146, 180, 182, 184, 217, 221
started 8, 161
starting 9
start-up   225
stated 120, 140, 149, 182, 187, 251
statement   3, 10, 82, 86, 143-144, 171, 173
statements   11, 25, 30, 39, 41, 57, 70, 73, 90, 102, 122, 138
status 5-6, 58, 124, 135, 171, 189-190, 196, 203, 207, 213, 215, 224, 239, 241, 245
statutory   225
steady 54
steering   135-136, 204
stocks 250
storage   184, 216
stored 137, 251
stories 32
strategic   51, 76, 91, 114, 127, 221
strategies   78, 93, 113, 169, 171, 193, 219-220
strategy   15, 34, 50, 77, 95, 104-108, 116, 129, 131, 195, 203, 207, 244, 250
Stream 58, 64
strengths   159, 172, 247
stretch 108
strict   61
strive   108
Strongly   10, 15, 26, 43, 58, 75, 91, 103, 216
structural   229
structure   3, 44, 88, 104, 117, 126, 144, 147-148, 163

structures 237
stupid 115
styles 180
subject8-9, 27, 66, 70, 72, 137
subjects 59
submitted 218
subset 16
succeed 53, 159
success 19, 24, 26, 37, 39, 41, 44-46, 53, 76, 82, 86-87, 94,
103, 107, 109, 113-114, 117, 126, 130, 132, 153, 161, 208, 213,
219, 228
successes 104
successful 63, 78, 93, 108-109, 121, 127, 132, 213, 254
succession 95
sufficient 131
suggest 215, 222, 233
suggested 96, 217
suitable 199, 225, 250
summarized 149
supervisor 226
supplier 79, 116
suppliers 29, 61, 64, 118, 152, 251
supplies 247
supply 54, 210, 251
support 7, 17, 93, 95, 100, 110, 113, 149, 162, 188, 193,
196, 207, 221, 231, 240, 246
supported 70, 194
supporting 85, 94, 136
supportive 153, 188
surface 96
SUSTAIN 2, 81, 103
sustaining 100, 159, 227
symptom 15, 53
system 9, 32, 71, 95, 116, 118, 138-140, 143, 149, 165, 185-186,
217, 221, 239, 241-242
systematic 49
systems 62, 64, 68, 73, 82, 86, 97, 143, 180, 221-222, 232,
242, 247, 250
tackle 53
tactics 219
taking 214
talent 67, 112
talents 121

CPSIA information can be obtained
at www.ICGtesting.com
Printed in the USA
BVHW041011200819
556236BV00011B/757/P